MURDER AT THE
NATIONAL CATHEDRAL
—— AND OTHER ——
HISTORIC D.C. CRIMES

MURDER AT THE NATIONAL CATHEDRAL

AND OTHER

HISTORIC D.C. CRIMES

ZACHARY G. FORD

THE
History
PRESS

Published by The History Press
Charleston, SC
www.historypress.com

Cover photo: Traffic scene, Washington, D.C., July 20, 1936. *Courtesy of the Library of Congress.*

First published 2025

Manufactured in the United States

ISBN 9781467158497

Library of Congress Control Number: 2024947488

Notice: The information in this book is true and complete to the best of our knowledge. It is offered without guarantee on the part of the author or The History Press. The author and The History Press disclaim all liability in connection with the use of this book.

CONTENTS

INTRODUCTION

From the 1930s through the 1950s, true crime reporting was truly in its classic or golden age. In this era, murder cases that caught the attention of the press were covered from every possible angle, often with daily articles. Many large cities had at least two major daily papers, allowing for even more comprehensive coverage. Any researcher or writer diving into these classic accounts will be impressed by the level of detail available to them but will also recognize that the degree of accuracy in coverage can be variable. Comparing one paper's article to another's on the exact same event will often reveal slight differences in details. Today's writer must evaluate the two and come to a logical conclusion as to which is more accurate; often a sifting and blending of the two accounts seems to arrive at the most accurate version of the story. Some papers also leaned more toward sensationalism than others or had slightly different areas of emphasis. But overall, the newspaper coverage of this era offers an excellent look at crimes that otherwise would be lost to history. The increasing takeover of television as the primary news provider for the masses eventually led to somewhat less comprehensive coverage of true crime in newspapers. Certainly papers continued to extensively cover major crimes, but the all-encompassing level of interest and detail given to true crime seemed to gradually fade away as the 1960s wore on. Offered here are seven true Washington, D.C. tales of murder from the 1930s to the '50s, preserved in the newspaper coverage of the time and buttressed by additional sources. I hope you find this foray into the classic age of true crime reporting to be a thought-provoking and informative look into Washington's past.

CHAPTER I

THE MAN WHOSE ARTERIES WERE HARD

A shriek echoed through the ninth floor of Washington, D.C.'s Houston Hotel early on the morning of October 12, 1935. Located at 910 East Street NW, it was a perfectly respectable place to stay in the nation's capital, but the story revealed that morning was anything but respectable. The screams awoke other guests at about 4:30 a.m., and one startled patron called the front desk, prompting night manager J.F. Sullivan to ride the elevator upstairs to investigate. Knocking on the door of room 903 and getting no response, he opened the door, but the chain bolt allowed it to open only slightly. He called into the room, "Open the door," and a male voice from inside replied, "Just a minute," but no one came to the door. Realizing that something strange was occurring, Sullivan told the occupant to open the door or he would "bang it in." Asking what was going on, the voice replied, "I can't stop this woman from screaming." Still he didn't come to the door. A young woman's head poked out of the room next door and asked Sullivan where the screaming was coming from; he tried to fob her off by saying it was from "way down the hall" and that she should go back to bed. Persisting, she asked if it was from the room next to hers, and he again told her to go to bed. She pulled her head back inside her room and closed the door. At this point, Sullivan decided to call for hotel manager J.C. Van Story, who came up to see what the matter was while Sullivan called the police. Peeking inside, he shouted for whoever was inside to open the door but got no further response. Policeman Horace Childress was assigned to a nearby patrol car with a radio and responded to the call from the Houston Hotel. He arrived and forced the door open, revealing a shocking sight.

A ROOM AND A BATH FOR TWO AND A HALF

Left: The Houston Hotel was respectable lodging in 1935, but it was also the scene of a bloody scandal. *Author's collection.*

Opposite: Willie Mae Wood was seduced by an older man but tried to turn the situation to her advantage, with disastrous results. *Author's collection.*

A past-middle-aged man clad only in his underwear and covered in blood was lying next to a young woman on the floor, his head resting on her chest. A bedsheet covered her body, and when Childress lifted the sheet to see if she was responsive, it revealed that she was likewise wearing only her underwear and was also covered in blood. It was clear that her throat had been cut. Not only was the bed next to them stained with blood, but blood was also sprayed over the wall behind the bed. The man mumbled incoherently and was bleeding from wounds on both arms as Childers got him up and took him into custody. As he was led out of the hotel, the bleeding man kept alternately muttering, "My God, have mercy on me," and, "She double-crossed me."

Police went to the room next door, where the young woman had earlier appeared; it did not have a connecting door to the murder room. Upon the police's knocking, seventeen-year-old Anne "Annie" O'Bannon answered the door and identified the occupants in the neighboring room. The dead woman was her cousin Sarah "Willie Mae" Wood. (She seems to have been universally called Willie Mae or sometimes just Mae; I will use "Willie Mae" or "Wood.") Up until September 26, she had been Willie Mae Fletcher; she was a newlywed. The injured man led away by police was William Reaguer, and both were from Culpeper, Virginia. O'Bannon was attending business school in D.C., where she lived with her father and stepmother. The teenager had quite a story to tell. At police headquarters, O'Bannon made an odd statement to reporters gathered to hear the latest scoop: "I have nothing to fear. I did no wrong. There is nothing I can say now which would help my cousin." It was not exactly a statement to reduce speculation from the press. Police had plenty more questions for O'Bannon, and she would remain in police custody until the fourteenth as a strange tale began to reveal itself.

Police escorted Reaguer to receive first aid at Emergency Hospital, where it was found that he had tried to cut his right wrist with a knife and had also tried to cut an artery on the underside of his left arm. Seeking an explanation for his bizarre behavior, Dr. Thomas Christensen checked for signs of drunkenness; he could smell liquor on Reaguer's breath but didn't think he was drunk. Reaguer "gave the wrong name" to Dr. Christensen, and when the doctor asked who killed the girl, he mumbled, "Wood did it." Dr. Christensen later recalled that "one minute he would say he wanted to die and the next minute would say 'take good care of me.'" He was acting so wildly as he shouted and moaned incoherently that he had to be restrained on a cot at the hospital, but after a few hours, his mental state began to clear somewhat. After the self-inflicted wounds were treated, Reaguer was sent to Gallinger Hospital. The hospital's full name, Gallinger Municipal Hospital Psychopathic Ward, left no doubt that doctors thought the man was not in his right mind.

Meanwhile, police looked more closely at the scene; the deceased "blonde and slender" young woman's head rested on a pair of men's trousers draped around her shoulders. The source of the blood splashed across the room

Willie Mae Wood lies in a modest, easily overlooked grave in Culpeper that bears her birth name, not the name that became so infamous. *Author's collection.*

was clear; the young lady's throat was cut deeply, nearly decapitating her. Coroner A. Magruder MacDonald arrived on the scene and stated the obvious when he declared it a "murder." The cut was done so neatly that onlookers thought it was done by someone with anatomical knowledge. Further examination by MacDonald found that "she evidently put up a terrific fight for her life. There were several gashes across her face, several deep gashes on her breast, and several cuts on her hand." Amid the blood spattered on the walls, bloody handprints were visible, starting shoulder high and lowering to the floor near the end of the bed. When police shook out the bloodied bedsheets, a two-bladed pocketknife came clattering out. It was apparent that the larger blade broke partway through the attack, and the smaller blade was evidently used to finish the job. An empty pint bottle of whiskey was also found in the room, as was the dead woman's pocketbook, which held a newspaper clipping about her recent marriage. Police went to Reaguer's car, parked in the nearby Washington Garage, where they found a loaded double-barreled shotgun, an almost empty pint bottle of whiskey and, most oddly, a hunting dog, which they turned over to the D.C. pound.

A *Washington Times* reporter tracked down Willie Mae's father, James "Jack" Fletcher, in Culpeper. He was a humble worker on Works Progress Administration road projects and a tenant farmer. Cruelly, the reporter was the one to deliver the news before authorities or family members could do so. Fletcher told reporters that "the law must take its course. She was such a cheerful, friendly girl. She always had a good word for everyone. I have known Reaguer all my life. I always thought he was a fine, honorable gentleman. But that can be changed just like that," adding a snap of his fingers. Almost sobbing, he continued, "I thought she was spending the night here in my house. I saw her as I went to bed. Now see what happened." The stress of the situation may well have contributed to Fletcher's demise in early April at the age of fifty-nine after an illness of a few weeks. Not surprisingly, Willie Mae's mother, Dolores, "swooned" and fell into a "state of collapse" when informed of her daughter's death. Like Willie Mae's parents, her new husband, Herbert, found out about the murder when a reporter called him about 8:30 a.m. on the twelfth. He then came to the D.C. Morgue to identify the body; he was reported to be "in a highly nervous condition" but kept his composure as best he could.

A portrait of William Reaguer began to emerge. He was a fifty-six-year-old undertaker from Culpeper, Virginia, and had two grown, married daughters, as well as a son who died in 1934. He and his wife, Bessie, had been married for twenty-five years. After growing up in Rappahannock County, he moved to Culpeper and over the course of twenty years became a respectable member of the community, belonging to the Baptist church, Rotary Club and Chamber of Commerce. Reaguer was described by a reporter as a prominent "citizen, undertaker, fisherman and huntsman." The Reaguers were prominent enough in the community to regularly show up in local newspaper social columns, and their daughter Elise's wedding in June 1934 was reported at some length in the *Washington Post*, where she was described as a "popular society girl." His son-in-law told the press that Mrs. Reaguer had an "open mind" about the emerging news but didn't intend to visit him "for the time being." However, she would end up supporting him throughout what was to come.

The strange situation became somewhat clearer at the coroner's inquest held on October 15. Reaguer was held at Gallinger Hospital under twenty-four-hour guard until the inquest but was reportedly in "good spirits." He was taken by police headquarters for fingerprinting and photographing before the inquest opened. More than a dozen witnesses testified at the coroner's inquest in front of relatives and friends crowded into the D.C. Morgue and spilling into the street. Reaguer declined to take the stand and sat silently but "occasionally smacked his fist onto an open hand which had one finger missing" (lost years before in a hunting accident). According to a reporter, he "looked more like a rugged, weather-beaten farmer" than a killer. Although Reaguer did not testify, Policeman Charles Burnett stated on the stand that the accused killer had confessed the previous morning at the hospital while Burnett was guarding him. In Reaguer's version of events, following a quarrel he and Willie Mae "went to bed together. About 4 a.m. she said she would rather die than argue all night" and then picked up a pitcher from the washstand to hit him. He saw that his pocketknife was lying on the bed, so he grabbed it, and as she jumped at him, "I cut her," as he simply put it. Hurting his story was the unanimous testimony from witnesses that the pitcher was unmoved from where it normally stood, not to mention the amount of effort it would take to nearly decapitate someone with a pocketknife. Some other statements that Reaguer made at the police station and hospital were ruled to be inadmissible since he had been advised by an attorney not to speak and only partially answered the questions that were asked of him. Sitting silently through the proceedings, Reaguer flinched at crime scene photos and "bowed his head" when the knife was shown.

Willie Mae's mother testified and confirmed what must have already been apparent: her daughter had been "going about with" Reaguer for several years despite her disapproval. Most subsequent testimony suggested that their relationship began when Willie Mae was sixteen and became "intimate," as papers delicately put it, when she was seventeen. Mrs. Fletcher stated that Reaguer gave Willie Mae a car, money and a ring but denied that Reaguer offered to buy her daughter another car if she broke up her marriage with Wood. She added that he threatened Willie Mae with a shotgun at the family farm shortly before her marriage. Nineteen-year-old Margaret Fletcher, Willie Mae's sister, said Reaguer had been a "frequent visitor" to their home, but the visits became less frequent after Willie Mae's marriage. When he visited, he would ask other members of the Fletcher family about Willie Mae's social life. In particular, he was interested in who her boyfriends were, and he would give family members money when they provided him with information about her. He made no secret about his desire for Willie Mae, for Margaret recounted how he would always talk about how much he loved

The D.C. Jail became the temporary home of William Reaguer and many other killers featured in this book. *Courtesy of the Library of Congress.*

Willie Mae and that "he wouldn't stand for her going out with anyone else." As evidence of this, he once waited at the Fletcher house until 11:00 p.m. when he heard that Willie Mae had gone out with friends and threatened to "choke the lungs out of" whomever she was with. His relationship with Willie Mae was not a secret in Culpeper. A friend testified later in the trial that Reaguer talked to him about Willie Mae, and he advised him several times to give her up; Reaguer would promise to but always went back to her. Only briefly was mention made of the fact that Mrs. Reaguer was aware of the affair after finding her husband and Willie Mae "in a compromising position," as a witness put it.

Willie's Mae husband, Herbert Wood, of Fairfax Station, also took the stand. A steam shovel operator for the Virginia Highway Department, Wood testified that he met Willie Mae in March 1935 when he boarded at the Fletcher house while working in Culpeper. He left in May but would return periodically to Culpeper to visit Willie Mae. The pair took a trip to Dayton, Ohio, to visit her uncle shortly before their marriage. Wood proposed on the Dayton trip, and a mere five days later, they were married back home and then took up residence at his parents' home in Fairfax Station. While in Dayton, Mae wired Reaguer for some money, and he sent ten dollars, so

The interior of the D.C. Jail was a far cry from the comfortable home life William Reaguer was accustomed to. *Courtesy of the Library of Congress.*

although Wood described his relationship with Reaguer as "casual" and said that he didn't know much about him, he knew that Reaguer was providing money to his intended wife. He admitted that he was aware of the past "peculiar relationship" between his wife and Reaguer, but she promised never to mention it after their marriage. He added that he knew Reaguer was "bitterly jealous." The Sunday before their marriage, the couple was at the Fletcher house, and Willie Mae informed her fiancé that she was going out with Reaguer in his car to tell him about the marriage. She returned, but Reaguer had not taken the news well and threatened the couple with a shotgun, telling Wood that "you'll not get Willie Mae or anyone else." Willie Mae's mother, Dolores, had to calm Reaguer down and persuade him to leave. Wood passed him on the street in Culpeper a few days later but didn't speak to him and never involved the police, so he must not have taken the threats very seriously. In response to a question, Wood "hotly denied" that he suspected his wife of still going out with Reaguer. When his wife didn't return to their Fairfax Station home on Friday night, Wood said that he drove to Culpeper and then to D.C. since he knew that O'Bannon spent most of her time there. When he couldn't find any sign of his wife, he spent the night driving the roads between Culpeper and D.C.

The audience was most interested to hear from "pretty, blond school girl" Annie O'Bannon. In short, she testified that Reaguer, irate over Willie Mae's marriage, forced the two women to accompany him from Culpeper to Washington, threatening them with a loaded shotgun. The full details of that strange evening would emerge at trial. The coroner's jury immediately gave a verdict after the evidence was heard. Reaguer was bound over for grand jury action immediately after the inquest and booked into the District Jail. An indictment for first-degree murder followed on November 6. A Third Criminal Court session was commenced to clear the court docket before summer recess. Justice Oscar Luhring presided over the trial, which was expected to last more than a week and see more than thirty witnesses called. Assistant U.S. attorneys Irvin Goldstein and Cecil Heflin were assigned to prosecute the case. Reaguer evidently had the money to hire a robust defense team composed of D.C. attorneys James O'Shea and, coincidentally, Alfred Goldstein, as well as local Culpeper attorney Burnette Miller. As jury selection began, O'Shea worked to keep all women and all fathers of daughters near Willie Mae's age off the jury, exhausting his twenty peremptory challenges, while the government used twelve challenges.

Going into the trial, there was no question that William Reaguer killed Willie Mae Wood; the defense readily conceded it. The defense aimed to save the undertaker from the electric chair by using an insanity defense. There would be two main parts of the defense: testimony to prove that he was clinically insane and testimony to show that Willie Mae's actions pushed Reaguer over the edge. A clearer picture of exactly what happened that night would lend some insight into the nature of Wood's and Reaguer's relationship. It would be up to Annie O'Bannon to fill in most of those details. Mrs. Fletcher was in the small second-floor courtroom, dressed in black and heavily veiled, along with Wood as O'Bannon took the stand. During her testimony, at times O'Bannon "shook almost to the breaking point" and nearly sobbed as she twisted a handkerchief around her hand but "never faltered" under O'Shea's cross-examination. She laid out the tale of what had occurred on October 11.

Annie was staying at the Wood house in Fairfax Station for a few days to recover from an illness. About 9:00 a.m. on October 11, the two girls, Mrs. Fletcher and two Fletcher sisters met in Fairfax. They went to D.C. to go car shopping, and the group returned to Culpeper that afternoon and then went to the Culpeper County Fair. After some time at the fair, Wood and O'Bannon returned to the Fletcher house before the others. Mrs. Fletcher had earlier said that Willie Mae originally intended to spend the night at the Fletcher house for the first time since her marriage, and when she said she was going back to Fairfax Station that night, she unsuccessfully begged her not to go. O'Bannon's trial testimony differed somewhat from what she initially told police. Earlier, she said she and Willie Mae left about 7:30 p.m. to catch a bus back to Fairfax Station. While they were waiting for the bus, Reaguer drove up and an argument began, leading to the girls missing the bus. Instead, he told them to get into his car and he would drive them to Fairfax Station. Now, O'Bannon testified that Reaguer actually drove up to the Fletcher house at about 6:00 p.m. Another Fletcher sister, Helen, was present, and Willie Mae had her tell Reaguer that she was not at home. Not believing her, Reaguer entered the house with a bottle of whiskey in his hand and demanded that Willie Mae speak to him in private. They stayed in one of the house's bedrooms for over an hour before O'Bannon told Reaguer the girls needed to catch the last bus to D.C. He told them to forget about the bus and announced, "I am going to take you both to Washington. I cannot give her up." O'Bannon still insisted that the trip was made "over their protests," but more evidence would emerge to make that claim questionable. The defense would seize on pieces of evidence like the extended conversation in the house that suggested the girls willingly went to D.C. with Reaguer.

Once the drive began, Reaguer supposedly began to threaten to kill Wood if she didn't give up her new husband and complained that she had played a "bad trick" on him, although O'Bannon said she initially thought the threats were a joke. He refused to stop in Fairfax and continued driving, ominously handling a double-barreled shotgun, and then started ranting about driving to Reno, Nevada, so Wood could divorce her husband. When Willie Mae asked him why he had a shotgun, he replied that "he could never tell who he was going to meet." To the follow-up question of whether it was loaded, he said that it was and added menacingly that he had more ammunition for it. He had a partially empty bottle of whiskey that he had clearly been imbibing from, and he insisted that Willie Mae have a drink, but she just touched the bottle to her lips to make him think she took a drink.

In his agitated state, he got lost as rain began to fall and stopped at a gas station to ask for directions; he warned O'Bannon that she better not try to trick him or escape. O'Bannon acknowledged that she did not try to get help from the gas station attendant, again suggesting that the trip may not have been as unwanted or frightening as she claimed. As they approached D.C., Reaguer abruptly forgot about his plan to drive to Reno and instead parked his car in the Washington Garage at 11th Street and E Street NW and then took the girls into the Houston Hotel at about 11:00 p.m. As they went in, O'Bannon assured Wood that she wouldn't leave her. Reaguer reserved two rooms at the front desk, but when he tried to register them, his hand was shaking too badly to write. He gave Willie Mae the pen, but her hand was shaking badly as well, so Annie took the pen and registered them as "H.L. Thomas and family of Richmond, Va." Would a kidnapped woman do that and then go upstairs with her kidnapper rather than write a message to the clerk? The defense certainly didn't think so. Hotel employees didn't detect anything strange about their behavior and assumed that they were father and daughters. O'Shea attempted to establish that Reaguer was "very drunk," but O'Bannon said he was "partially under the influence of liquor" but not "thoroughly intoxicated." The defense was hedging their bets by also trying to show that Reaguer's alleged intoxication was another reason why he couldn't premeditate a murder, while more than once prosecutor Heflin referred to evidence disputing his drunkenness.

When they arrived at the rooms, Reaguer told Annie to go out and buy some whiskey, but she protested that it was late and she was underage, so he just ordered ice water up to his room and told the girls to come in. O'Bannon complained that they were tired, but Reaguer insisted that Wood stay, although he said O'Bannon could go to the other room. Willie said she wanted to take a shower and asked Annie to stay in the room while she did so. Reaguer acquiesced but first went into the bathroom to see if there was a way she could escape. Satisfied, he told them they could escape only by jumping out of the ninth-floor window, and Willie Mae was able to take her shower. While she was in the shower, Annie began to write a letter to Margaret, Willie Mae's sister, but Reaguer said "he would rather I wouldn't write from the hotel, as we weren't supposed to be there and I crumpled up the letter." He asked her if she and Wood were trying to get away from him and begged her not to let Willie Mae "double cross him." When Willie Mae came out of the shower, she wanted to go to the other room, but Reaguer said he wanted to talk with her alone. It was about 1:00 a.m., and according to O'Bannon, Wood said "all right and told me to go on." As O'Bannon left, he told her that he knew they were trying to escape and he would kill Willie Mae if either of them tried to get help. Before leaving, she told her friend to knock on the door five times before entering so she would know it was her. For a woman supposedly terrified for her life, she rather oddly went to bed without any effort to get help and soon fell asleep.

About 4:30 a.m., O'Bannon was awakened by seven or eight loud, "frantic" screams, "just like a shriek….I could not tell for a minute where I was….They were so loud I couldn't tell who was screaming or what direction they were coming from." She "reached across the bed to see if Willie Mae was there" and then went for the telephone in the room but heard the elevator arrive and knocking begin down the hall. Bizarrely, she insisted that she "did not connect the voice with that of her cousin," despite the fact that she had last seen her supposedly being held captive and threatened. After a brief conversation with the man doing the knocking, described at the beginning of the chapter, she got dressed because, rather puzzlingly, "I felt that if something hadn't happened, I ought to get out of there before something did happen."

Recall that O'Bannon began to write a letter in Reaguer's hotel room, only to be stopped by him. The police had collected the crumpled-up letter as evidence, and now the defense used it to further suggest that the girls were not being held against their will. In the letter, O'Bannon wrote, "Dear Sue, here we are on the first leg of our flight. Willie is taking a shower and I'm just thinking about you," seemingly implying that there was indeed some sort of strange plan for Willie Mae to leave her husband to be with Reaguer. When O'Shea asked her what she meant by that statement, she didn't clarify matters much by replying that she simply intended to convey that getting to D.C. meant that they had completed the first step of their journey home.

But if they were kidnapped and in fear of their lives, why would she think they were just going to drive home the next day? O'Bannon added another layer to the story when she had earlier admitted that she and Willie Mae went with Reaguer "as much from fear that Wood would learn they were with Reaguer as from terror of Reaguer himself." By "Wood," she meant Herbert Wood, Willie Mae's new husband.

The defense brought employees from the Washington Garage, where Reaguer parked his car, to the stand. They put a very different spin on what happened that night. They testified that the "small coupe" arrived at about midnight with Wood driving and Reaguer sitting in between her and O'Bannon. Both Reaguer and Wood seemed to have been drinking, and "their clothing was in considerable disarray." Willie Mae asked employee William Perry where the hotel was and then turned to Reaguer, saying, "Let's go. The sooner we get up there the more time we'll have together." Perry said that he found a nearly empty pint whiskey bottle and a shotgun behind the front seat and a hunting dog in the luggage compartment. Charles Mullen, the garage night manager, said the pair "rearranged their clothes" after getting out of the car. All O'Bannon could do when brought back to the stand was deny that any drinking occurred or that any clothes were disarranged, although what motive Perry and Mullen had to perjure themselves is less than clear. As the day's testimony ended, one of Reaguer's daughters rushed up to him as he left the courtroom and embraced him.

Despite O'Bannon's best efforts, the jury must have had a strong suspicion that Willie Mae, if not a willing participant in the trip, was at least not in mortal fear of her life. Further testimony about the financial gifts that she received from Reaguer strengthened the impression that she was perfectly willing to manipulate her "sugar daddy." One can't forget that Reaguer started a completely inappropriate relationship with a teenage girl, but over time she was apparently willing to take advantage of the situation. Testimony at the inquest already revealed that Reaguer gave Willie Mae a car, a diamond ring and money. At the trial, further details emerged, and Margaret Fletcher acknowledged that Reaguer gave her mother $50 toward the purchase of another car but denied knowing that Reaguer had also paid the family's grocery bills. (Reaguer later said that he would give the family up to $100 a month for groceries and other items.) She also clarified that Reaguer had not bought Willie Mae just one car, a Plymouth, but in fact she had traded in the first car for a nicer one, a Chevrolet, and he paid the difference. He then gave her a second car, but she sold it shortly before her marriage and pocketed the cash. One gets a rather unsavory impression that while the Fletcher family may well have abstractly disapproved of the relationship, they didn't do much to end it and shut off the financial benefits they received from Reaguer. Of course, for a family headed by a tenant farmer and road worker during the Great Depression, perhaps it is easy for the modern reader to judge the family too quickly.

All of this built up to one of the defense's main points: Reaguer was satisfied to break off the relationship when Willie Mae was married, but she insisted on maintaining it for her financial advantage. The defense said that Reaguer "broke off" the affair after the marriage, but "she wouldn't leave him alone." A longtime friend saw Reaguer on the Sunday after Wood's marriage; he said she was happy that she was married so he could end the relationship, as "it was a burden on him," and added, "I'm glad she's off my neck." Another friend confirmed that Reaguer told him, "I am glad she is married. I have been trying to get out from under [her] for two years. I hope they live happily." This friend added that Reaguer had no hard feelings over Willie Mae selling the first car he gave her, saying that "it is all right with me." A third friend gave an almost identical account, saying that Reaguer told him after the marriage, "I'm not resentful. He's a fine young man. I'm glad to get her off my hands. I gave her the car, and it was hers."

Alan Rosenthal, a Culpeper merchant who worked across the street from Reaguer's undertaking business, provided evidence that Willie Mae willingly continued to see Reaguer after her marriage. He testified that he saw Willie Mae visit Reaguer's business several times both before and after her marriage. In fact, Rosenthal said that he saw her come out of Reaguer's building at about 8:00 a.m. on October 11, the day of the murder. She obviously had gone there just before her car shopping trip, and as we shall soon see, it was to follow up letters she sent to Reaguer seeking money for the car. Reaguer must have been tormented about how to proceed. Shortly before meeting the girls that fatal night, Reaguer visited his friend Dr. Granville Eastham and read him the letters from Willie Mae. Reaguer was worked up enough by the situation that Eastham gave him a "small quantity of a drug to quiet his jangled nerves." Defense lawyer Burnette Miller said the drugs on top of the whiskey Reaguer consumed that day was like putting nitroglycerin on top of a bomb. Following Reaguer's meeting with Dr. Eastham, witnesses in Culpeper saw him leave town at about 7:30 p.m. He said he was going to the Culpeper fairgrounds, about a mile away, one presumes to confront Willie Mae. This route passed the Fletcher home, and he must have seen her at home with O'Bannon, setting in motion the bizarre events that followed.

The letters that Reaguer read to Dr. Eastham showed that Willie Mae wanted another car and proved the defense's contention that she "pursued him with endearing letters." In fact, the defense produced two very important letters from Willie Mae to Reaguer, written less than two weeks after she was married. Reaguer's lawyers were only too happy to read the letters to the court. O'Shea began reading the letters in "a soft voice which contrasted with his former rasping tones."

The first letter, written on October 7, read:

> *Hello, dear. Came up this morning to get my tooth fixed. Sure wish I could have seen you, but Herbert was with me. I will be able to go to Washington either Wednesday or Thursday, so if you can possibly leave enough money with Mama for the down payment, or as much as you want to pay. The first payment will be about $50. I won't be able to see you before then, and that will be the only chance I will have to go to D.C.*
>
> *After they get the car, I will be able to see you real often. Will be ready to go either Wednesday or Thursday. Hope you will be able to get the money. Be good and think of me until I see you. Tonight is good ole Monday night. Wish you could be here so I could be with you.*
> *Bye, darling*
> *Willie*

A second letter written on October 9 read:

> *Dear darling: Where on earth were you yesterday? I drove around I know 50 times. I wanted to see you so bad. I am tired of this married life. Could you possibly get the first payment on the car by tomorrow? It will be about $50. Herbert is going to sell his car and I won't have any way to get up there to see you. If you can give me another car I will leave it at home and Mama can drive down and get me every evening after Herbert leaves. Please darling, give me another car, 'cause you know I love you as much as ever. If you really want to see me, you will do this once more. Mama is going to come to Washington tomorrow, and if you give her the money I will meet her at Fairfax and drive it back, then I will be able to see you. This is the last time that I am going to ask you. I know you will do it for me and I won't have to ask you any more. Hope to see you real soon, dear.*
> *Love always.*
> *Willie*

As O'Shea read out the love letters, Herbert Wood sat in the back row of the courtroom, "half smiling, with a cynical twist to his face." The letters held the explanation for the October 11 car shopping trip the Fletchers made to Washington. The Fletchers were evidently confident that Reaguer would continue to fork over money to Willie Mae. The fact that Willie Mae was trying to wheedle more money out of Reaguer suggests that Mrs. Fletcher was telling the truth when she denied that Reaguer offered her a car to break up her daughter's marriage, but who can say if Willie Mae perhaps dangled that enticement out herself at some point. Having established that Reaguer may well have cracked under pressure from Willie Mae's attempts to continue their affair, the defense team then attempted to prove that he was clinically insane. His attorneys described how he changed over several years from an "affable, genial man into a brooding, nervous and dazed person" and brought a series of witnesses to prove the point. The defense theory was that he had "been suffering for several years from advancing hardening of the arteries, with marked mental deterioration." It surely must be one of the few insanity-by-arteriosclerosis arguments ever made in a courtroom, and his attorneys spent considerable time describing his medical history.

A parade of character witnesses including an attorney, bank cashiers, Baptist and Presbyterian ministers, neighbors, an insurance agent, merchants and a trial justice were brought to the stand to describe a man who had gone from respected citizen to one allegedly not in control of his mind. One witness testified that "his reputation for peace and quietude has always been good," and the overall point was to stress that he had been mentally normal before medical issues and a tragedy sent him into a spiral of insanity. It was quite apparent that sympathy in Culpeper leaned more toward Reaguer, despite the fact that he had seduced a sixteen-year-old girl. There was probably a social class issue at play that shaped his peers' attitudes. Willie Mae, from a poor family, was perceived as leeching off the socially higher William Reaguer. Through it all, his wife, "quiet and cultured," did not testify but told reporters that "we have known of Mr. Reaguer's mental condition for some time."

Culpeper doctor O.K. Burnett testified that in 1932 he treated a "rather drunk" Reaguer for a "severe head wound" caused by being hit with a pipe. The defense could not have been entirely pleased when he stated that Reaguer received the wound at the hands of another man in a fight over Willie Mae. Reaguer complained of severe pain in the back of his head "as if he had been hit with a hammer.…[H]e was wild and unmanageable and I couldn't do much with him." The good doctor's solution was to administer an opiate "to quiet him." Burnett believed that he was suffering from a hardening of his arteries and a likely cerebral hemorrhage. Burnett sent him to the University of Virginia Hospital in Charlottesville, where, during a ten-day stay, he was diagnosed as having a blood clot on the brain that caused a small stroke. Dr. Burnett was called again in May 1935 when Reaguer complained of "headaches, nausea, and dizziness…and said he couldn't sleep at night," which Dr. Burnett said were "all symptoms of hardening of the arteries," although one would think they might be the symptoms of a great many medical issues. (To eliminate one possible source of medical issues, doctors who conducted routine tests the day of Reaguer's arrest testified that he was not suffering from any "social disease" he may have picked up from a woman.) By this time, Burnett had noticed a change in Reaguer's mental state as well, noting that he could not exercise proper judgment and was not himself, as he was not as friendly and did not "greet people as cordially as he formerly did."

Besides hardening arteries, testimony also suggested that Reaguer's mental state was affected by the death of his son Earl, a Virginia Tech graduate, who died on August 29, 1934, at the age of twenty-five. His early death was due to pulmonary tuberculosis with influenza as a contributory cause. Reaguer was described rather cryptically by a character witness as being "inordinately fond" of Earl, who he was training to take over the family business and who he often hunted with. Major John Karrick of Rixeyville spoke about Earl's death on the stand; he was a boyhood friend of Reauger's and testified that "he had been jovial and greeted his friends heartily" until his son's death, when he seemed to "withdraw from the world and to dislike meeting people." While he had sat silently through most of the trial, alternately wringing his hands and covering his face with them, Reaguer burst into tears at the mention of his son.

One of Reaguer's daughters related an incident when he got up in the middle of the night in his nightgown, drove his car up the road with no lights on and came back fifteen minutes later with a "terrified, wild, startled look in his eye." She added that he had increasing difficulty running his business, and she got a laugh from the audience when she was asked about how well his business was doing. She replied that it always varied and it was "hard to say about the undertaking business. They don't die every day, you see." Even Reaguer's dog was referenced to show his owner's mental state. One witness related an incident where the dog approached Reaguer and he said, "Come, old boy, you know there's something wrong with master, don't you?"

Rosenthal, a Culpeper merchant, offered a rather odd example of Reaguer's supposed insanity when he said that Reaguer was a "poor fishing companion" on an August 1935 trip even though he'd been an "enthusiastic fisherman all his life." Reaguer was such a dedicated fisherman that Rosenthal said that his lack of interest in fishing was a sure sign of insanity for him. In perhaps an even more feeble example, Rosenthal said that the fishing group went bowling on the trip, and everyone but Reaguer burst into laughter when Rosenthal got his thumb stuck in a bowling ball. On the trip, Rosenthal awoke one night to find Reaguer groaning and holding his head in his hands while muttering, "I must be going crazy." Rosenthal concluded, "I thought he was nuts at times." He also unintentionally amused the courtroom audience when he related an incident where Reaguer insisted he had bought a pair of suspenders at Rosenthal's store when he hadn't and kept trying to pay for them. Prosecutor Goldstein asked Rosenthal, "Couldn't it have been you who forgot?" and he "emphatically replied, 'No, sir. When I ring up 25 cents on the cash register, I remember about it.'"

A town official who had helped Reaguer collect business debts testified that he increasingly found that Reaguer would send him to collect debts that had already been taken care of. Eventually, he stopped helping him because he had become so confused with his business dealings. The defense also brought Harry Bywaters, a Culpeper pharmacist, to the stand, and as evidence of Reaguer's declining mental health, he related that he was often confused over money matters. Specifically, he came into his drugstore over a dozen times to pay bills he had already paid a day or two before. He added that Reaguer was at his drugstore on the night of October 10, the day before he began his strange ride to D.C., and he "seemed gleeful.…[H]is face was flushed and he had a wild look in his eye." The prosecution brought the Culpeper sheriff, two bankers and a businessman to testify that Reaguer had not been acting oddly, but it was not enough to counteract the points made by the defense, weak as some of them were.

Now, the defense shifted into a more clinical discussion of Reaguer's supposed insanity. They brought Dr. Antoine Schneider, a Georgetown neurology professor, and Dr. J.H. DeJarnette of Western State Hospital in Staunton to testify. Schneider said he was sure that Reaguer was insane at the time of the murder, and he was under the "impression" that he still was. Based on two examinations of Reaguer, Schneider made sure to tie his diagnosis into the key element of the defense case when he stated that Reaguer suffered from "arteriosclerosis of the brain, with psychosis." The effects of Reaguer's hardened arteries allegedly altered his mental state into the realm of insanity. Dr. Raymond Foxwell, a "specialist in nervous and mental diseases," was also brought to the stand by the defense. He related that Reaguer had told him that on the night of the murder he and Willie Mae "were very depressed and agreed to commit suicide," and then Willie Mae somehow managed to nearly decapitate herself before Reaguer cut his own wrist. Reaguer added that when he woke up, he thought he was in Culpeper. A reporter drily observed after hearing this unlikely tale that the "doctor's testimony was sketchy and few details were given." Testimony from Dr. Schneider related that Reaguer later told him the suicide pact story was "just a dream." Dr. Foxwell also stated that Reaguer had an "extremely suspicious nature" and on his second visit with Dr. Foxwell had to be convinced that he was the same doctor that had examined him before. Reaguer also continually wept during the mental exam.

O'Shea used a not-uncommon tactic in questions of sanity and formulated a twenty-three-page summary of Reaguer's life and actions, all posed as one very lengthy question. The intent of the multi-page question was to elicit confirmation that the question described an insane man. He posed the question to his expert witnesses, who of course confirmed that it showed Reaguer to be insane. The fact that Dr. DeJarnette had never actually examined Reaguer did not stop him from not only declaring Reaguer insane but also launching into monologues that earned several rebukes from Justice Luhring. Prosecutor Irvin Goldstein, tired of Dr. DeJarnette's responses, asked him if at the time of the murder Reaguer knew what a knife was. Dr. DeJarnette acknowledged that he would have. Goldstein then asked if Reaguer knew that a knife would kill Willie Mae. The doctor had to again acknowledge that, yes, he would have known that too.

The prosecution brought their first expert witness, Dr. D. Percy Hickling, a "nationally known alienist," to the stand. Hickling said that after examining Reaguer twice, he concluded that while he was "not normal from a medical point of view," he was "certainly not insane from a legal point of view." In response to a point raised by O'Shea that Reaguer was in a mental "borderland," he argued that there was no such thing as a borderline case when it came to insanity; everyone is on one side of sanity or the other. He added that "Reaguer is sane and the hypothetical man described in the hypothetical question is sane." In response to the defense claim that Reaguer was an alcoholic, Hickling turned the point around and said that due to his heavy drinking, he was "almost impervious to the effects of alcohol."

Prosecutors also brought their own Georgetown professor, Dr. Richard Thibadeau, who testified that Reaguer was sane and simply had been faking insanity and malingering. He noted that Reaguer could remember testimony from the first day of his trial and what he had for dinner, but when asked to repeat an address as part of a mental evaluation test, he claimed he couldn't do it. Dr. Thibadeau used a blackboard to illustrate arteriosclerosis and said it wouldn't have made him insane. Twenty-first-century medicine supports Dr. Thibadeau. Cerebral arteriosclerosis is a legitimate condition, and it can lead to some of the symptoms that Reaguer experienced, such as headaches and confusion, but it does not remotely lead to psychosis or an altered mental state where someone would meet any legal definition of insanity.

A reporter observed that the trial's "principal forensic fireworks" occurred during closing arguments. Irvin Goldstein said the defense wanted to show Willie Mae as "trash" and Reaguer as a "leading citizen." The letters were introduced simply to "damn and blacken her character so you gentlemen will conclude she deserved to be killed....He started her off when she was 16. He defiled her body, ruined her soul, and now tears from her the last shred of her reputation, holding her up naked for the morbid gaze of the crowd." Working himself up to a fever pitch, Goldstein thundered, "The wraith of Willie Mae Wood stands behind me, one arm pointed at the defendant and with eyes turned toward you, demanding the vengeance of the law." Heflin added, "He was the man who started the girl on the downward path. Whatever may be said against her falls on his shoulders." He added that arteriosclerosis was normal in a man his age and was irrelevant; the defense offered an insanity defense only because they couldn't think of anything else.

During the defense's closing arguments, Burnette Miller said, "We realize we must tread softly on the actions of the dead." Of course, that in itself was really meant to highlight Wood's apparently questionable actions. The defense pointed to garage employee Perry's testimony as the "beacon illuminating the last acts and thoughts of Willie Mae," namely that she willingly accompanied Reaguer to the Houston Hotel. O'Shea said there were two Reaguers, the old, respectable one and the new one, whose "mind snapped under a terrible cerebral hemorrhage and grief and drink. The man whose arteries were hard, and who was desperate." Defense attorney Goldstein covered all of his bases when he told the jury to find Reaguer insane if he didn't know between right and wrong, "if he did not know that the acts he performed constituted the crime charged" or if he knew it was wrong but was "unable to resist." He also said that if they found he was so drunk that he couldn't form deliberate intent, they couldn't deliver a first-degree murder conviction. Finally, he brought up a dubious-sounding legal concept when he "emphasized the legal maxim that good reputation alone is sufficient to create reasonable doubt."

After closing arguments wrapped up and the lawyers conferred with Justice Luhring about his charge to the jury, O'Shea asked Luhring to allow for second-degree murder or manslaughter verdicts, which he agreed to do. A first-degree conviction carried a mandatory death penalty, while a second-degree verdict could mean anywhere from twenty years to life in prison. The jury received their charge just before 3:00 p.m. on April 30; it would not be an easy decision. By 10:30 p.m., no verdict had been reached, and the men were locked up for the night. The jury returned to the courthouse at 8:40 a.m. the next day and deliberated until 10:10 a.m., when they sent word that they had reached a verdict. None of Reaguer's family was present, but news of the decision resulted in a rush of other observers crowding into the courtroom. Asked by Alfred Goldstein how he felt, Reaguer said, "Well—you know—nervous, of course." The nine hours of debate resulted in a conviction for second-degree murder. As the verdict was read, Reaguer seemed unconcerned with the proceedings. Not quite hearing what the jury foreman said, he asked one of his attorneys what was said, nodded at the answer and calmly walked out. A reporter noted that his lawyers showed "obvious satisfaction" at the verdict, and they announced that they did not intend to appeal.

Reaguer had been on suicide watch, and a bathrobe cord and broken spoon were previously discovered and confiscated, but his mood improved after the verdict. As it sank in that he was going to live, "his joy became more and more apparent." He told reporters, "I sure am glad I didn't get the chair….Just look at those trees. I tell you, the world never looked as beautiful to me as it does now." At Reaguer's sentencing, Luhring gave him the maximum life sentence, saying that "when the jury failed to find him guilty of first-degree murder, they gave him all the consideration to which he is entitled." Reaguer departed in early May to begin his sentence at Lorton Workhouse, which one paper disapprovingly noted was referred to as the "Country Club" prison.

Bessie Reaguer did not long survive the ordeal, dying at home on December 29, 1936, from a heart attack after being weakened by the flu. Her obituary noted obliquely that she was the "wife of W.H. Reaguer, formerly of Culpeper." Reaguer evidently made arrangements for his undertaking business to continue while he was incarcerated, for in July 1937, the Reaguer-Stradley Funeral Home was chartered with Reaguer as president. His old defense attorney Burnett Miller represented Reaguer in the action. Death

William Reaguer lies apart from his mistress in another Culpeper cemetery, buried alongside his family. *Author's collection.*

came for William Reaguer on February 23, 1945, at the Lorton Workhouse Hospital. A local paper carried an understandably bland obituary; one of his pallbearers was his old friend Dr. Granville Eastham, who had done his best to help him on the stand. The primary cause of death given on Reauger's death certificate was pulmonary tuberculosis, the same as his son Earl, with an oddly appropriate contributory cause: generalized atherosclerosis.

CHAPTER 2

DISORDERLY CONDUCT

Shortly after 6:00 a.m. on November 27, 1935, Washington, D.C. police received a phone call reporting that the body of a woman had been found; they needed to come to 918 4th Street NE right away. When officers arrived at the two-story rowhouse, they found thirty-five-year-old Elizabeth Lynch lying fully clothed on her kitchen floor. Her head pointed toward the door, and she lay on her left side, partially lying under a table. A broken maple chair was next to the body, and a .38-caliber snub-nosed revolver lay at her feet. The revolver was loaded, and one of the cartridges had been expended. It was immediately apparent that the woman was dead, and the cause of death was likewise obvious, for there was a bullet entrance wound in her left cheek. Based on the pattern of bloodstains on the front of her brown dress, investigators thought that Lynch likely was "sitting erect" when shot. Police called for Coroner A. Magruder MacDonald to come to the scene; he arrived and spent over an hour examining the body and crime scene. He found that the fatal bullet ranged upward into Lynch's brain, resting near the back of her head. There were no powder burns on her face; MacDonald and police were immediately convinced that this was no suicide. Someone had shot her from a far enough distance that no powder burns resulted. MacDonald determined that rigor mortis had set in and that Lynch had died at least three hours earlier, putting her death at no later than 3:00 a.m. and most likely at about 2:00 a.m. He found only a few bruises on Lynch's legs; otherwise, there was no evidence of injury on her body. Tests of her blood and stomach revealed that she had recently consumed alcohol, but not enough to reach intoxication.

Coroner A. Magruder MacDonald (*second from right*) features in many of the stories related in this book. *Courtesy of the Library of Congress.*

If they hadn't recognized the name of the man who reported finding the body, police quickly realized who they were dealing with. William "Dutch" Kappel was a thirty-four-year-old man with a long criminal history in D.C. (His age was variously reported through the years; the birthdate information he gave on at least one document conflicts with census information, so he was evidently happy to leave it murky.) Kappel acknowledged that he lived at Lynch's residence, and neighbors told police that they assumed Lynch and Kappel were married. More startlingly, Kappel admitted that the revolver found in the kitchen belonged to him. According to Kappel, he and Lynch had gone to a restaurant at about 7:00 p.m. on November 26 along with a friend named Leo Cullen and another unnamed woman. He accompanied Lynch home in a taxi at about 11:30 p.m. after an argument, and she refused to let him into the house. He returned to the restaurant and stayed there with Cullen until it closed at 2:00 a.m. They visited a roadhouse in Maryland, only to find it closed, and then went to another club, where they stayed until nearly 6:00 a.m. He then returned to Lynch's house and discovered her body lying on the kitchen floor, fetched Cullen from his house two blocks away and called the police at about 6:40 a.m. Or so he said. Police had heard enough to take Kappel into custody for further questioning, and they also held Cullen, a thirty-one-year-old pressman for a local newspaper who resided nearby at 718 4th Street NE. As Kappel and Cullen were put into a police wagon, Cullen threatened photographers and kicked angrily at them while Kappel lunged at one and said, "You take my picture, you ———, and I'll break that camera over your head."

As is so often the case, it is the victim who remains more of an enigma than the perpetrator. Lynch was a switchboard operator at the Potomac Electric Power Company service station located at 10th Street and Florida Avenue NE and had worked there for ten years. She was divorced and was described by one paper as "an attractive brunette whose hair was streaked with gray." In May 1933, "charging misconduct," she filed divorce proceedings against her husband, Ager Goodwin, a marine, and she named a co-respondent in the divorce. The divorce was granted in June 1934. As noted previously, she was living with Kappel in what was evidently a common-law marriage or perhaps something more temporary and casual. Both of her parents had passed away within the year or so before her death, and she inherited the family home upon the death of her father. A sister, Mary Agnes Brooks, lived in D.C. and was devastated by the news of Elizabeth's murder. (She would petition to administer her sister's estate as the closest living relative. Her request noted that Lynch's home was valued at $2,047 and her personal property at $3,805.) Lynch's decade-long employment as a switchboard operator had evidently been satisfactory, although police were told of an ominous incident that occurred on November 2, several weeks before her murder. The otherwise reliable employee failed to show up for work, and it was eventually discovered that she had been "beaten about the face in a fight at home." She related to a friend that she had gone to a movie without Kappel and then to the home of a mutual acquaintance, accompanied by a female friend. Something that occurred there prompted a violent attack on her, presumably from Kappel, that left her with blackened eyes and a bruised face. Of particular interest to detectives was a friend's comment that Lynch reported not only being beaten up but also being threatened with a gun in a bathroom. However, friends said that she did not appear worried when she went to work on the morning before her death, and she never involved the police.

Police investigators, headed by Detective Sergeant John Dalglish, looked into Kappel's story that he had gone with Lynch and Cullen to a restaurant in the 1200 block of New York Avenue on the night of the murder. Witnesses confirmed that the three were seen there until 11:00 p.m. or so and that they were drinking. An argument erupted between Lynch and Kappel over another woman Kappel was paying attention to that night, and Lynch left the restaurant alone but was soon followed by Kappel. All of this generally matched Kappel's story. The cab driver who took Kappel and Lynch home never seems to have been traced, but police were very interested in finding the taxi driver whom Kappel claimed picked him up at 4th Street and H Street, near Lynch's home, after he had been refused admittance by Lynch. The cab then took him back to the restaurant, where he and Cullen continued their partying. Kappel could not recall the name of the cab company, but police eventually tracked down a cab driver who gave only his last name, Botts, to reporters. (A second taxi driver also turned up who said that he picked up a man at the same location and gave a vague story about taking him "downtown," but nothing much seems to have come of his story.) Botts said that he picked up a man at the time and location described by Kappel and dropped him at 12th Street and New York Avenue, also as described by the suspect. The driver put the time of the pickup at 12:20 a.m. The distance between the restaurant and Lynch's house was about a ten-minute drive, so assuming that Kappel and Lynch did leave the restaurant at 11:30 p.m., that makes an arrival time of about 11:40 p.m. Presuming a wait of several minutes on the cab when he left, that left a window of twenty-five or thirty minutes when Kappel and Lynch could have been left alone. Detective Dalglish had to consider how precisely to interpret the estimated time of Lynch's death. If he strictly accepted MacDonald's conclusion that the death occurred around 2:00 a.m., then having a window of opportunity at around midnight did not prove that Kappel was the killer, especially if he could prove his claimed alibi that covered that time frame. However, given the vagaries of estimating the time of death, a true death time of two hours earlier would seemingly not be outside the realm of possibility either.

Examination of the broken chair in Lynch's apartment showed that the back and seat had been cracked and splintered and several rungs were knocked loose. The chair was strongly made, and police did not think that it could have been broken just by Lynch falling on it. At some point, it must have been thrown or otherwise used as a weapon, leaving several pieces scattered across the kitchen. One piece of the chair lay next to the kitchen sink, while another rested in a saucepan sitting in the sink and a third lay under a gas heater. Another piece was partly under Lynch's body, certainly suggesting that it was broken before her demise. The kitchen stove appeared to have been struck by something, and detectives thought that the chair hit the stove rather than Lynch herself. There was no other damage evident in the kitchen; the house was being repainted and the walls were being hung with new wallpaper, and that process hadn't been disturbed. Police fingerprint experts found a "slight impression" on the gun but never said whether it matched Kappel's fingerprints. If it did, it would not really help the case, as Kappel had freely admitted that the gun belonged to him. Dalglish said he asked Kappel if he picked up the gun to identify it, and Kappel replied that he hadn't "since he knew better than to put his hands on it." A pair of leather gloves also lay next to the sink, but Dalglish found them too small to fit Kappel.

In the absence of major developments in the case, the press reminded readers about William Kappel's colorful past. Police described Kappel, six feet tall, stocky and ruddy, as a "petty racketeer" and noted that he had been in custody twenty-six times since 1913, with a wide range of charges. His list of arrests makes for an interesting insight into the crime scene in the first decades of the twentieth century. His criminal record began in 1913 with, of all things, a charge of violating child labor laws. The sentence was quite reasonably suspended for the eleven-year-old, although one wonders why he would be charged in the first place rather than just his employer. Charges of housebreaking led to a stint in the National Training School, followed by another stint on the wonderfully archaic charge of "incorrigibility." As his age increased, so did the seriousness of his crimes as he graduated into various charges of assault with a deadly weapon, drunk and disorderly conduct, transporting whiskey, destruction of private property and "breaking glass in street." Two assault with a deadly weapon charges dated from 1926, but in what would become a pattern in his life, both were ultimately not prosecuted. He did face more minor convictions, being fined multiple times for his continual disorderly conduct as well as a specific charge of being "disorderly in a house." (For the more pure-minded readers, please note that a "disorderly house" used to be a common euphemism for, at best, a gambling joint and, at worst, a brothel.) Kappel was frequently referred to in newspaper accounts as a "well-known local sporting figure," with "sporting" clearly referring to gambling. In just the year before Lynch's death, he faced charges of assault, carrying a concealed weapon and destroying private property, but all were dismissed. At the time of his arrest, Kappel bizarrely gave his occupation as iceman, which one presumes must have been a flippant remark to police or reporters.

Leo Cullen was no angel either and had a criminal record that dated to 1918, when he was put on probation by a juvenile court for disorderly conduct. Six years later, he was sentenced to pay ten dollars or serve ten days for petit larceny, and he forfeited collateral six times on disorderly conduct charges and once for an intoxication charge. Police tallied eighteen arrests in total for Cullen, mostly drunk and disorderly charges with a bit of petty larceny mixed in. Also insightful into Cullen's idea of a good time are charges for "joy riding," indecent exposure and his own "disorderly in a house" charge. Cullen and Kappel were obviously buddies by August 1933, for on the twenty-sixth of that month, both men were charged with assault on one Nick Vlahos.

In fact, Kappel had been involved in a mysterious death before. In November 1928, Kappel and several others attended a party at a friend's apartment on 14th Street for some drinking and fun. At some point that night, John "Jack" Grady ran afoul of a poorly designed glass skylight, which sat in the middle of the apartment, covered with mesh and surrounded by a low balustrade. Grady went crashing through the skylight and landed on the floor of the apartment below, no doubt much to the surprise of the residents. Kappel and another man gathered up Grady and drove him to a local hospital at 2:30 a.m. and then sped off without leaving their names. Police investigated the suspicious death and tracked down Kappel and four other of the party attendees and took them into custody, while another remained on the lam. All of the arrested parties insisted that Grady had been drinking and was sitting on the balustrade around the skylight when he simply leaned backward too far and fell to his death. The whole crew at the party were shady characters, and it was noted that Kappel was "well known in the circles in which Grady moved," and those circles involved illegal booze and gambling. A police informant relayed rumors that there was a fight at the party over a craps game and Grady was thrown through the skylight, but investigators could not prove anything. Police did find an impressive cache of eighty-eight quarts of alcohol on the roof of the apartment but nothing that could tie Kappel or anyone else to a possible murder. In January 1929, Kappel and the others were released without charges, and a newspaper noted that "nothing ever seems to come of the arrests of Arthur Kappel." (Newspaper articles would occasionally use his middle name, Arthur. Presumably a man involved in crime would have had reason to shift between names.)

Illustrating how prolific his record of arrests, but not convictions, was, at the same time that Kappel was being held in the Grady investigation, he was questioned about his alleged assault on a Maryland constable as well as a charge of driving with a revoked license. In November 1929, police raided several gambling and bootleg joints, and Kappel was one of those arrested at a speakeasy where admittance required pressing buttons at two doors to gain entrance to a secret gambling room. But again, nothing much seems to have occurred in the way of punishment. His next brush with the law occurred in December 1930, when Kappel and an associate were arrested after a brawl at the Green Gables roadhouse in Maryland ended up with a man injured by a gunshot and his brother, a policeman, beaten up. Although Kappel was indicted the next year, witnesses conveniently could not be found, and the case never went to court.

Kappel was on the receiving end of gunfire in yet another bizarre incident. In December 1932, Kappel and some friends attended a dance marathon and then retired to one of their apartments for some drinking. Soon, a local hospital received a call to send an ambulance to the apartment, and the responding doctor found Kappel lying on the floor with a bullet wound to his groin. Police arrived and were immediately suspicious when they saw two men's overcoats and hats lying on the floor, although Kappel was the only man present. Two women were there, but they insisted that they were not in the room when Kappel was shot and had no idea what happened. For his part, Kappel insisted that he had accidentally shot himself, which was a difficult proposition to support when police were unable to find a weapon in the apartment and Kappel could not explain where it had gone. Also militating against his self-shooting claim was the fact that a second round had been fired and lodged into a wall. Police noted that attempts to question the three people in the apartment were "handicapped by the effects of liquor." Although Kappel stuck by his story that no one shot him, police tracked down the owner of one of the men's overcoats, John Costello, and charged him with assault with a deadly weapon. But since Kappel was not cooperative, there was no way to continue with the prosecution. Finally, although not linked to William Arthur Kappel in papers, one can't help but wonder if one Arthur Kappel arrested at the Canadian border in December 1933 trying to smuggle $4,000 of gold across the border was our man.

All of this, of course, left little doubt that Kappel might just be the sort of man who could end up shooting someone during an argument, but that didn't help investigators close the case. While the police continued to investigate, Attorney Charles Ford was hired to represent both Kappel and Cullen. They were released to his custody on the night of November 30, pending their appearance at the upcoming coroner's inquest. That same day, Lynch's funeral was held, followed by burial at Mount Olivet Cemetery. Although no date had been set yet for the inquest, Ford said that he would not try to have the pair released until the police had a "reasonable chance to complete their investigation." The coroner's inquest eventually met at the D.C. Morgue on December 3. Not a great deal of new information arose during the inquest, but the medical and physical evidence of the case was reviewed, and several of Kappel's friends testified that he was at the New York Avenue restaurant until 2:00 a.m. on Wednesday and then visited several other places with Cullen until 6:00 a.m. Papers noted that one of the witnesses was Denny Sothern, a former National League baseball player who ran the restaurant. Sothern testified that Kappel left the restaurant as he described at about 11:30 p.m. and then returned about forty-five minutes later and "took a snooze." Cullen also took the stand to confirm the story. Some of the corroboration of Kappel's story seems to be a bit too perfect, and papers noted that several witnesses "appeared somewhat uncertain" of the time he left and returned when cross-examined by Assistant District Attorney Allen Krouse. Krouse also noted that Kappel's and Cullen's more recent accounts of the night seemed to have shifted the timeline to better suit their needs. It was certainly important for them to have their whereabouts accounted for around the 2:00 a.m. death time posited by Coroner MacDonald, as well as minimizing the time around midnight when Kappel was alone with Lynch at her home. Despite the testimony of his friends, at the end of the inquest, Kappel was held for grand jury action. Cullen was never charged in the case and was released. The grand jury presented an indictment for first-degree murder on January 6; arraignment followed on the tenth, and Kappel entered a plea of not guilty.

But a trial would never happen. As with so many other times in Kappel's life of crime, prosecutors entered a decision of *nolle prosequi*, meaning that the charges were not being prosecuted but could be potentially resurrected in the future. Assistant U.S. attorney Roger Robb told reporters that they simply had insufficient evidence to proceed with a trial. District attorney Leslie Garnett had conferred with Robb, who then quashed the indictment. Garnett said that at the time of the indictment, prosecutors felt there wasn't enough evidence to prosecute, so the case was delayed while the prosecutor's office and police tried to get more evidence. When it became apparent that no more evidence would emerge, Garnett could not justify holding Kappel over the court's upcoming summer recess. Kappel was released from custody on June 26. Major Ernest Brown, superintendent of police, told reporters that there would be no further investigation unless new evidence appeared and added that "we have no more evidence." Reading between the lines, it appears that investigators were sure that they had their man. Major Brown said he was "surprised" when informed that Kappel was released but denied that he had ordered an investigation into the circumstances of the case being dropped. Defense attorney Charles Ford said that criticism of the DA's office for dropping the case were "outrageous" since "lawyers all know that if a person once is brought to trial and acquitted, he never can be tried again for the same alleged offense." However, Ford was quick to add that his client was innocent.

Did Kappel kill Elizabeth Lynch? Almost certainly, but the prosecutors were likely correct in not proceeding with the case. Although common sense pointed toward Kappel's guilt, proving guilt beyond a reasonable doubt was a very different matter. It does not seem likely, but it is admittedly possible, that another person showed up at Lynch's house that night shortly after her argument with Kappel, obtained Kappel's revolver and murdered her. Having quarreled with Lynch at the restaurant over another woman and, by his own admission, following her home, it is not difficult to imagine a fight erupting between Kappel and Lynch with the chair hurled at Lynch. With Lynch perhaps on the ground after dodging the chair, "sitting erect" as investigators believed, that could explain the bullet ranging upward through her cheek. Since it was evidently fired from a distance, an accidental discharge during a struggle doesn't seem particularly likely, but perhaps in waving his gun around, it went off accidentally, or it could have been completely deliberate. The fact that the pistol was left at the scene is rather odd; surely an experienced criminal like Kappel would have thought to dispose of it, particularly given his experience with the 1932 shooting incident. Maybe he thought police would think it was a suicide, or maybe he just panicked. Given his admission that he owned the gun, even had fingerprint evidence emerged, it would not have been useful at trial to convict him. His alibi for the supposed time of death is not entirely convincing, and moreover, MacDonald's estimation of death was likely too specific and limiting. It would seem that, once more, Kappel dodged a conviction that he rightfully earned.

In the aftermath of the case, the press received a surprise when they found out that there was in fact a Mrs. Kappel. Upon hearing that her husband was released from custody, Nellie Kappel called the police to request protection from her spouse. Officers on patrol in the area were told to "keep an eye" on her house at 1119 Orren Street NE. The fed-up Mrs. Kappel filed for "absolute divorce" on August 24, stating that she had married her husband in March 1931 and she left him due to "cruelty" in July 1934. According to Nellie, he never supported her, and she always paid the rent. Further, "his abusive, cruel and inhuman" conduct caused her to be "in mortal fear of her life." The 1934 D.C. city directory certainly seems to confirm her statement that she was the one supporting the marriage, for it does not list an occupation for William, but it lists an intriguing occupation for Nellie. She worked as a "phone operator" for the electric department, which begs the question of whether she was a coworker of Lynch's, who worked as a switchboard operator for an electric company. Perhaps it was just a coincidence, but if the two were coworkers, it would explain how Lynch and her no-good paramour may have met.

As events proved, "Dutch" Kappel could not stay out of trouble, but the legal system still could not seem to get him into a courtroom. He and an associate named Harry West were arrested in June 1937 when police heard "through the grapevine" that a local numbers racket had been robbed of $1,500. It seems that they decided to "round up the usual suspects" and brought Kappel and his compatriot to a lineup. Oddly, the people viewing the lineup were several liquor store owners who had been robbed in recent months. Newspaper coverage does not clarify why they would be trying to identify people supposedly involved with robbing a numbers racket, unless their "liquor stores" were really just a front for such operations. The lineup led nowhere, and police were actually in the strange position of not having a complainant for the supposed crime; a numbers racket was not exactly going to reach out to the police and report that they had been robbed. In other words, the police couldn't even be sure that a crime had actually been committed, so Kappel and West were released without charges.

The law finally caught up with Kappel in 1938 with what papers tallied as his thirty-seventh arrest. He and an accomplice were indicted for a November 21 holdup of two "well-known local sportsmen." Kappel and his associate ambushed the racketeers at gunpoint in the garage of one of the victims' homes and then jumped in the victim's car to make their getaway. The police soon tracked down Kappel, and he again looked to attorney Charles Ford to keep him out of jail. Ford filed for a mistrial based on the admittance of certain evidence, but Justice James Proctor rejected the request and simply had the jury ignore the questionable evidence. Kappel insisted it was a case of mistaken identity, but one of the victims testified that he had met Kappel several times and definitely knew it was him. On April 25, 1939, Kappel was convicted, and despite an appeal, on May 5 he was sentenced to prison for the first time in his long criminal career. Justice Proctor sentenced him to a term of two to eight years' incarceration. Several months later, his accomplice was arrested for another robbery and admitted to his role in the robbery with Kappel.

The 1940 census found Kappel in Lorton Workhouse, but he was evidently out by February 1943, for he dutifully filled out his draft registration card at that time. He was living in tiny Tall Timbers, Maryland, with his mother, although he cryptically listed "none" as his mailing address. He apparently stayed out of trouble for his remaining years, which admittedly were few, as he died on February 23, 1948, in Lanham, Maryland, and was buried in Suitland, ending his days as a man who likely had gotten away with murder.

CHAPTER 3

WHAT COULD I DO BUT SHOOT HIM?

The overwhelming majority of murders involve people who would otherwise be lost to history, those who briefly made their appearance in the public consciousness and then faded back into anonymity within the larger community. But on rare occasions, society's most prominent members can find themselves embroiled in murder. Such was the case in 1944, when Washington, D.C.'s most famous lawyer entered the headlines for a very unexpected reason.

Robert Ingersoll Miller was an icon of the D.C. law scene, spending decades as the "most picturesque" lawyer in town, according to a reporter. That newsman also noted that he was given to "making long, impassioned pleas in the most insignificant cases" and generally ensured that he was always the center of attention. Perhaps his namesake, a famous nineteenth-century orator, provided inspiration. Miller, sixty-seven in 1944, the year that concerns us here, started work as a janitor in a D.C. police station, decided to go to law school and rose through the legal establishment. He carefully cultivated his eccentricities, among them always carrying what he called his "lucky money," supposedly given to him by "gypsy" clients. In a 1921 newspaper profile, he claimed that he always won cases that occurred on Friday the thirteenth and noted that he was born on that day. (Perhaps giving additional insight into his personality, when asked his opinion on jazz, he sniffed that "there is little enough good music in the world without the jazz band coming in.") More ostentatiously, he was known to carry around a $1,000 bill, pull it out and casually clean his eyeglasses with it. He owned several racehorses, one bearing the name Not Guilty. But he also backed up his theatrics with success in the courtroom, taking virtually any client willing to pay him and usually getting the desired "not guilty" verdict. He held the record for the fastest disposition of a murder case in D.C. history when a client shot his brother-in-law at 9:00 a.m., attended a coroner's inquest and received a verdict of justifiable homicide by 1:00 p.m. On another occasion, Miller defended a man on a drunk driving charge who was found in a wrecked car, reeking of whiskey. Despite the overwhelming evidence against his client, Miller said he would simply have him tell the "plain truth." The man stood up and explained to the jury that an unknown man had accosted him on the street on the evening in question, held him at gunpoint and ordered him to drink a pint of whiskey. Perhaps stunned by the audaciousness of the crazy tale, the jury acquitted him in five minutes. Despite his flashiness, Miller was known to often pay the fines of clients in the seemingly uncommon times when he lost a case. He happily represented Black clients, and the *Washington Afro American* referred to him as "one of the race's best friends," specifically referring to a 1937 case where he saved a Black man from the seeming inevitability of the electric chair. Clearly, Robert Miller was a complex man.

Miller was long involved in Republican circles in Washington and counted numerous politicians as personal friends, with Charles Curtis, vice president under Calvin Coolidge, as a particularly close friend. A reporter noted that his "manner and mustache are reminiscent of Teddy Roosevelt, whom Miller greatly admired." In fact, Miller was a Republican delegate at the 1912 and 1916 conventions, although evidently his views could be a bit idiosyncratic, as he was also the president of the Roosevelt Republican Club in 1932, campaigning for Democrat Franklin Roosevelt. Miller went through at least one tragedy in his life with the death of his wife, Katie, in February 1928. He did not mourn for long, as he remarried in October of the same year to Marguerite Kane (sometimes spelled Margarette), a woman over two decades his junior who would shape his life in ways he couldn't imagine at the time. By the 1940s, Mrs. Miller had become increasingly close to another prominent member of Washington society, Dr. John Lind, the fifty-seven-year-old chief medical officer at St. Elizabeth's Hospital, the most well-known mental institution in Washington. Employed there for thirty-one years after attending Georgetown and George Washington Universities, Lind often wrote journal articles on psychiatry and frequently testified as an expert witness in court. He was known to keep in good shape, for, as a newspaper vividly described, he often had to "fight off attacks by the demented." Personally, he was reported in the press to be a popular bridge player and a "fluent and witty conversationalist who was always in demand at social gatherings." An insinuating but rather dubious-sounding society column quoted a St. Elizabeth's nurse, who referred to him as "the famous and brilliant Dr. Lind....All the nurses think he's *wonderful*!" He also had the rather unusual hobby of writing songs for children. He was a widower who lost his wife in 1937 and was a father with three grown children.

Marguerite Miller met Dr. Lind through her husband's legal circles and became his patient for obscure reasons, but around 1939, her relationship with Dr. Lind turned into a full-blown affair. A rather unlikely vixen, described in a paper as a "buxom silver-haired matron," she gave her birth year as 1902, but it appears that reflected a subtraction of three years off her true age. She was not entirely happy at home, as she was known to complain about the Millers' house and how she wanted a more expensive one. In truth, she was on to something, for their house at 1314 8th Street NW, while respectable, did not really reflect the lawyer's true wealth and was described by reporters as having an old-fashioned, dark Victorian interior. While personally flashy, evidently Miller's household arrangements were much more modest. Marguerite Miller's relationship with Lind was never much of a secret, although her husband claimed to have not learned about it until July 1943. Lind's children were aware of the relationship, and his daughter often pleaded with him to break off the affair, with no success.

The affair boded ill for all involved, and matters would come to a head at Woodward and Lothrop's, for many years the most prominent department store in Washington. On Monday, February 21, 1944, it hosted a drama that captivated Washington for months. Lamar Johnson, a porter at the store (papers ensured that readers knew he was "colored"), stood at the employee entrance near the corner of 11th Street and G Street NW, about fifty feet down from a larger public entrance. At about 1:20 p.m., he was working on polishing brass fixtures. He would recount what he saw in the next few moments multiple times over the coming months. As he later told it, he noticed a man in the store hanging around the employees' entrance. Moments earlier, other store employees had seen the same man suspiciously hiding behind racks of coats in the store and seemingly spying on someone; he was reportedly seen rather ludicrously parting a rack of coats to peek through, and an employee became suspicious enough to call the store detective. However, the man headed toward the entrance on 11th Street. There, Johnson later said he saw the man light a cigarette, puff it a few times and then stamp it out as he paced nervously. Johnson asked him if he was

Left: Prominent lawyer Robert Miller and his wife, Marguerite, found themselves in the midst of 1944's most sensational court case. *Courtesy of ACME Newspictures.*

Below: Dr. John Lind is seen examining string "art" made by one of his mental patients at St. Elizabeth's Hospital. *Courtesy of the Library of Congress.*

waiting for someone and told him he could stand at his place at the employee door so he could have a better view of the street. Just then, Johnson saw a black sedan driven by a man pull up in front of the store after driving northbound on 11th Street. A woman in a fur coat approached the car and entered the front passenger side. The nervous man suddenly brushed past Johnson, went through the door and pulled open the car door the woman had just closed. He seemed so firm in purpose that Johnson thought he was a detective about to arrest the woman. The man pulled something out of his right pocket, and a struggle began with the driver until two shots rang out. The man ducked back out of the car and the woman who had just entered also exited and tried to pull him away from the car. In what would prove to be his most controversial statement, Johnson believed that he saw the man then reach into his left coat pocket, pull out something white and place it on the front seat of the car.

Navy chief machinist mate William Stearns, on his honeymoon with his bride, Irene, also in the navy, saw the shocking scene play out. The car, still in drive, rolled forward toward the intersection with G Street, and Stearns leapt into the front seat from the passenger side, hit the emergency brake and turned off the ignition, trying to avoid the obviously dead man at the wheel. Stearns looked for the other man and saw that he had walked a short distance down 11th Street and then turned around and came back. Stearns grabbed the apparent killer's arm, but he offered no resistance. Dozens of other stunned bystanders out on their lunch break stopped to see what was happening. Some thought they had heard the woman in the car shout something during the scuffle between the men; one witness thought it was "Not that…no…not that!"

Another man, attorney Frederick Thuee, walked past the store at that moment and saw the same scene play out and later recalled events much as Stearns did. However, he knew exactly who was involved. He immediately recognized the man driving the car as Dr. Lind, whom he knew personally. He also knew the woman in the fur coat was Marguerite Miller and the man forcing his way into the car was her husband, a man he considered a friend. Thuee was thus shocked when Robert Miller's struggle with Dr. Lind resulted in two gunshots. Approaching Miller, the bewildered Thuee told him that he was sorry that he had to witness what had just happened. The only response Miller made was to ask whether he saw Lind pull a gun on him. Marguerite Miller, despite having blood splashed over her fur coat, stood by, oddly calm.

The Woodward and Lothrop building still looks over the spot where Lind's car was parked in the immediate foreground. Miller stepped out of the now-closed employee entrance door to the left of the main entrance. *Author's collection.*

Policeman Ernest Dickerson was directing traffic one block over at 11th and F Streets and heard what sounded like two gunshots. He immediately headed in the direction of the shots and saw people clustered around a car. Before he could even look inside the car, Miller came up and declared, "That's Dr. Lind. I shot him in self-defense. He pulled a gun on me. Look in the car; he's got a gun in there." After relieving Miller of the .38-caliber Smith and Wesson revolver he had just used, Dickerson looked into the car and saw an obviously deceased man slumped in the driver's seat; he had one bullet wound to his chest, and a bullet wound in his head bled freely. Further examination would show that there was an entrance wound on the right side of the skull and an exit wound through the left temple. On the front passenger seat, Dickerson saw a large white envelope, stained with blood, and reached for it, but Miller excitedly told him not to touch it without placing something around it. Had decades of criminal law made him think of fingerprints, or was something else at play?

Detectives arrived on the scene and examined the bloody envelope; inside was a .32-caliber Iver Johnson pistol. The revolver had two live rounds, two expended shells and two empty chambers in the cylinder. Given that the pistol was concealed in the envelope, Miller's statement about a gun being in the car immediately struck police as suspicious. Underneath the envelope was a freshly laundered white handkerchief that bore the monogram "M." It was certainly a suggestive monogram. Also on the front seat was a small shopping bag with a brassiere that Marguerite Miller had exchanged at the store. Deputy Coroner Richard Rosenberg performed the autopsy on Dr. Lind and found that Lind was shot in the chest first, and the gun was in contact with his clothing at the time of the shot. The gun was about two inches from Lind's head when the second shot went into his skull and then exited out of his left temple. (Rosenberg was a student of Lind's when he taught at Georgetown University, so it must have been an unusually personal autopsy to conduct.) The round that transited Lind's skull was found by police on the street as they were collecting evidence on the scene.

Robert Miller experienced a new side of the legal world when he was held overnight without bail in the local police precinct. He already had a de facto defense team: his own employees Joseph McMenamin and James Hughes. (Always booked with clients, he had two cases scheduled for the twenty-third that he dispatched an assistant to cover.) He soon added another prominent lawyer, H. Mason Welch, to the defense team. Miller remained in good spirits. As Miller left the police station the next morning for his bond hearing, he shook hands with police officers and joked with news photographers that he wanted a dollar apiece for the photos. Some eyebrows were raised by the public when Miller was granted bond later that morning. Amid accusations of preferential treatment for the prominent lawyer, the judge who granted the bond acknowledged that his release on bond was unusual under those circumstances but perfectly legal. Miller's attorneys insisted that he was in such poor health that he might die if kept in custody and pointed out that such a prominent citizen couldn't successfully escape town and avoid detection. Assistant U.S. attorney Charles Murray tried to fight Miller's bond and unsuccessfully requested a bench warrant to bring Miller to immediate arraignment, but this was denied based on Miller's physical health; Miller's personal doctor told the judge who granted bond that he had extremely high blood pressure and couldn't stand "undue excitement." While there almost certainly was some preferential treatment occurring, Miller had in fact been hit by a car while crossing a street several months before and had also evidently suffered a heart attack, so he did have genuine health concerns.

There was no delay in holding the coroner's inquest; it began that day, February 22. Miller attended the inquest but did not testify; the only concern he voiced was over what his wife's reaction might be at the verdict. The police guards showed an unusual degree of respect and deference for the accused man, following him at a discreet distance. There was no question that Miller had killed Lind, so a grand jury convened on February 24. Miller again attended the hearing without testifying, although after hearing porter Lamar Johnson's story of him nervously smoking, Miller angrily told reporters that Johnson "was a damn liar. I don't smoke and at no time was I in the store." Five other store employees eventually went on record testifying that they saw Miller inside the store, although Miller was supported on the more minor smoking point by acquaintances who testified that he was not a smoker. Miller's first comments on the murder scene had suggested self-defense, and he made sure to plant that idea in the heads of reporters when he memorably told them, "I just went over to the car to tell my wife to get out. Then that bastard said he'd blow my brains out. What could I do but shoot him?" Marguerite Miller likewise attended the grand jury hearing, bizarrely wearing the same bloodstained fur coat she had worn on the day of the murder. Meanwhile, Dr. Lind was buried on February 24 in Cedar Hill Cemetery and in his will left his dining room furniture and two tapestries to Marguerite Miller.

An indictment on a first-degree murder charge inevitably followed on the last day of February. The judge now had little choice but to discontinue

Above: Coroner A. Magruder MacDonald (*left*) asks a question of murder witness U.S. Navy Chief Machinist Mate William Stearns at the coroner's inquest. *Courtesy of AP Wirephoto*.

Opposite: Judge Ben Moore of West Virginia is seen leaving the courtroom with his wife. *Courtesy of AP Wirephoto*.

Miller's bond following his formal arraignment. One can presume Miller's status meant his trial was fast-tracked, with a start date of May 15. Since his arraignment, he had been residing in the District Jail infirmary. Juror selection did not prove to be particularly controversial, with the two sides only using twenty-nine of the forty challenges available between them. Eleven men and a solitary woman were selected. (After the trial began, a juror had a heart attack and was replaced by the alternate juror.) One juror did not make the cut after opining that "the wrong person was shot," meaning Marguerite Miller. Two other prospective jury members were released for rather odd reasons: one had installed the electric chair at the District Jail, and one was an assistant funeral director who helped to bury Lind. Justice Ben Moore, a West Virginian brought in to ease the D.C. caseload, would helm the trial. The presence of Judge Moore was fortuitous, for Miller's long association with Washington legal circles led many to speculate that it would be almost impossible to find a judge in D.C. who wouldn't have to recuse themselves based on their prior associations with Miller. Assistant U.S. attorney Charles Murray would prosecute, aided by colleague Daniel Maher. Miller retained his team of Welch, McMenamin and Hughes. While the trial was supposedly

held in the Municipal Court Building rather than the District Courthouse since more seating was available, the courtroom was described as small, with a capacity of fifty spectators.

As the trial began on May 15, Miller looked thin but healthy, although at one point during the trial he said he thought he was going to faint and smelling salts had to be administered during a recess. He appeared greatly interested in what each witness had to say and throughout the trial would periodically use the pince-nez attached by a ribbon to his coat to look at documents. It was probably no surprise to anyone what two main lines of defense Miller's attorneys would take: self-defense and insanity. A few articles did make explicit what any observer knew, that "weighing heavily on the jury will be the implications of a third line of defense, the 'unwritten law.'" This was the age-old argument that a husband more or less was justified in killing his unfaithful wife's lover to preserve his own sense of honor. While it could not explicitly be used as a legitimate legal defense, anyone sitting on a jury in 1944 would have the thought in the back of their mind. Ultimately, the trial would continue through May 31.

Both of the Millers had their actions on that day carefully reconstructed. Testimony from one of Lind's coworkers indicated that Marguerite Miller called for Lind the day of the murder; he was not in the office, but she left a message for him to return her call, and he did so, presumably coordinating their meeting that day. The Miller family maid said that Marguerite Miller left home at about 1:00 p.m. after speaking to her husband on the phone. Marguerite later confirmed the phone call on the stand and said that she had called her husband to let him know that she was going to Woodward and Lothrop's to exchange a brassiere that didn't fit, obviously not mentioning her intended rendezvous with Lind. The twenty-first began like any other day for Miller, and he spent the morning defending a client on a drunk driving charge. While at the courthouse, he made small talk with U.S. attorney Edward Curran, a man we will meet in the next chapter, about Miller's recent trip to Florida. He received the phone call from his wife at about 1:00 p.m., telling him about her plans to go to the department store. Suspicious, he then made a call of his own to St. Elizabeth's and found that Dr. Lind was not in. Putting two and two together, he headed out of his office and boarded a streetcar. Only Miller could say why things boiled over on February 21 and why he chose that day to resolve his marital issues; perhaps even he didn't really know. An attorney friend, Harry Harth, was on the same streetcar and greeted Miller but found him to be distracted and acting strangely. The normally talkative Miller practically ignored Harth and only grunted in response to Hart's attempts to make conversation, other than saying that he was going to Woodward and Lothrop. Harth and a court clerk on the streetcar then watched as Miller got off at the intersection of 11th Street and F Street. Miller then proceeded to his fatal encounter with Dr. Lind.

The prosecution did its best to prove that Miller had placed the envelope with the gun on Lind's front seat as a premeditated way to make it look like

Lind was armed and dangerous. The defense, of course, set out to prove that Lind was in the habit of carrying around a pistol and represented a genuine threat to Miller. As we shall see, their goal was to show that Miller thought that Lind was reaching for his weapon. Department store porter Lamar Johnson was brought into court to testify that he did see Miller place a white object into the car, and one George Ferguson, a physiology instructor at George Washington University, was brought to the stand to confirm that he saw Miller reach into the car a second time. However, the defense eventually brought seven witnesses to respond who swore that they didn't see Miller with anything white. Johnson admitted that the number of pedestrians on the sidewalk partially blocked his view, although the same could be said of the other witnesses. The defense attempted to further shake Johnson's credibility after he testified that there was ten to fifteen seconds between the two shots. Welch snapped his fingers with about a second between snaps and asked Johnson if he was sure the timing wasn't more like that. Johnson stuck with his timing and said the whole episode lasted one and a half to two minutes, a rather unbelievable length of time for the brief scuffle and shooting. Other witnesses would give more likely time estimates, with the scuffle probably taking thirty-five to forty seconds and only a second or two between shots. Intriguingly, another witness, Henrietta Willis, testified that after the shooting, she saw the Millers converse for a moment, and then Mr. Miller leaned back into the car like he was going to pull something out, but his wife stopped him. Was this him placing the envelope in the car? Or had he done so and was having second thoughts? Or what about the handkerchief with the "M" monogram? Perhaps he realized he had inadvertently left it in the car and was going back to retrieve it.

The issue of fingerprints on the envelope would be discussed at various points at the trial, but no real answer ever emerged. A police fingerprint specialist testified that neither the murder weapon nor the gun in the envelope had any identifiable prints on them. The expert was able to retrieve a single fingerprint from the envelope. It didn't match Lind or Miller. The FBI ran the print against their fingerprint files and found no match. There was a cryptic reference at the trial that "other persons who might possibly have had contact with the envelope" were tested, also with negative results. One important person the print was definitely not compared to was Marguerite Miller. Prosecutor Maher requested her fingerprints for a comparison, but she declined upon advice of her counsel, and Maher could not legally compel her to give the prints. Miller's secretary, Katherine Townsend, likewise refused a fingerprint test, but she was brought on the

The three members of Miller's defense team examine the infamous envelope. *Courtesy of ACME Newspictures.*

stand by the defense to testify that there were not any similar white envelopes in Miller's office. If Miller's fingerprint had been identified on the envelope, the prosecution certainly would have presented it as definitive evidence of him planting it, but presumably the defense could have argued that Miller happened to touch the envelope during the scuffle with Lind. Even had Marguerite Miller consented to a fingerprint comparison, it wouldn't really have helped the defense, since she freely admitted to being in the car on multiple occasions and could then testify that she knew that the envelope held Lind's gun, whether she knew that to be true or not.

The white handkerchief found under the envelope likewise yielded no significant evidence. Miller eventually admitted that it was his handkerchief, but he always insisted that he had no idea how it got there. Of course, the prosecution's conclusion was that he had accidentally left it there when placing the envelope and gun in the car, but there was no real way to prove it. The fact that it was under the envelope likely prevented the defense from claiming that it had fallen out of Miller's pocket when he struggled in the car, but they certainly could have advanced the argument that his wife happened to have one of his handkerchiefs on her and that's how it wound up on the front seat.

The FBI's new Washington, D.C. forensics lab did their best to find a fingerprint match to the envelope but were unable to do so. *Courtesy of ACME Newspictures.*

The defense team eventually brought forward fellow attorney Archie Shipe as an important witness regarding the mystery gun. He testified that while working on a court case that involved Dr. Lind as a witness in 1939, on three separate occasions he saw Lind with a manila envelope that held a book, papers and a dark-colored revolver. He clarified that the gun had a "blue steel" finish, and when Welch held up the gun found in the envelope, Shipe gave him the answer he was looking for: yes, the gun he saw was "about that color and size—very similar to that." Conversely, the prosecution tried to show that there was no evidence that Lind ever owned a weapon like the one in the car. Unfortunately for them, another layer to the gun story emerged: a .32-caliber pistol had been found in a dresser drawer at Lind's house. It was not identical to the type found in the car, but the defense was certainly happy to at least show that Lind owned a similar weapon. Dr. Lind's son William was given leave by the army to attend the trial and testified that to his knowledge, his father only owned one pistol, the one found in the dresser drawer. He had owned it for many years. One of Lind's daughters also took the stand to relay substantially the same information. The prosecution also argued that since the gun in the envelope contained two live rounds, two expended rounds and

A detective displays the pistol found in the envelope as he testifies. *Courtesy of AP Wirephoto.*

two empty chambers, it didn't make much sense for Lind to carry around a partially loaded gun like that. Of course, the argument could be turned around that had the gun been planted, Miller would have wanted it to be full of live rounds to make it look as threatening as possible.

The defense also sought to show that Lind's physical actions indicated that he was reaching for the gun and that Miller's self-defense response was logical. Even if the gun in the envelope was Lind's, Miller obviously couldn't have seen it, so the best the defense could do was show that Lind was reaching for the weapon. Frederick Thuee was brought on the stand to testify about the struggle he saw in the car. Welch mimicked a motion of someone reaching for a gun while they were seated, and Thuee agreed that Lind's movement looked like that. Welch tried to go even further and asked Thuee whether it appeared that Lind was reaching for a gun, but the prosecution raised an objection. Several other witnesses were asked about the struggle, and the overall impression created by the defense was that Lind's movements did indeed look like a man reaching for a gun by his side. More trial time was taken up after the defense presented a witness who claimed to have seen Lind move a pistol from one pocket to another at a restaurant on the Saturday before the shooting. The prosecution brought in three St. Elizabeth's employees to testify that Lind was at the hospital at the time that the gun sighting supposedly took place. The restaurant's owner testified that Lind and Marguerite Miller did dine there on that Saturday, but the witness

Dr. Lind's son William was placed on leave by the army to testify at Miller's trial. *Courtesy of ACME Newspictures.*

was not at the restaurant until later in the day than the couple. Overall, the supposed witness did not look very credible, and the defense wasn't able to add much to their case.

Besides trying to show that Lind had a gun in his possession, the defense also needed to explain why Miller was walking around with a pistol in his pocket. The story presented by his attorneys was that he had owned the pistol for many years but had taken it to his legal office so he could get what we would today call a concealed carry permit. He claimed that he had been "yoked" recently (a 1940s term for being mugged) and needed the gun for self-protection. He supposedly talked to the police about the matter and was told that those weren't sufficient grounds to get the permit, and Miller then dropped the matter. On the twenty-first, he was thus just bringing the pistol back home and happened to have it in his pocket. The prosecution brought in witnesses to testify that while Miller had indeed been mugged, it had been many months earlier, and it didn't make sense why he would suddenly decide he needed to carry around a gun. The prosecution also raised the excellent point of why Miller didn't just write down the gun's serial number for the paperwork rather than lug it around.

The prosecution brought Dr. Watson Eldridge, a coworker of Lind's from St. Elizabeth's Hospital, who described at least three conversations where Marguerite Miller discussed divorcing her husband, who was threatening her and Lind. According to Eldridge, Marguerite said she had "religious scruples" about divorce (although evidently not adultery). Eldridge also testified that Marguerite Miller freely admitted to spending money on Lind, particularly part of $18,000 she inherited, and she reiterated that her husband would kill her and Lind if he found out about the matter. Of course, this was an important point for the prosecution, for they wanted to show that Miller had been threatening violence against Lind, and not the other way around. Defense attorney Welch turned the testimony against Dr. Lind as best he could, asking Eldridge if Marguerite Miller was visiting Lind at the time because he was actually at St. Elizabeth's as a patient due to the fact that "he was drunk and had been drunk for days" and needed to "get sobered up." Eldridge denied that was the case, so Welch then asked if Lind was indeed there as a patient. Eldridge dodged the question as best he could, saying that he "was not my patient," and then had to admit that Marguerite Miller had checked Lind into the hospital. Welch continued laying out the scenario he was trying to prove: was it true that Lind was there to be treated for alcoholism and no records were kept? Eldridge denied that and said Lind was treated for high blood pressure and diabetes, but Welch didn't give up. He asked whether those were not symptoms that were "a direct result of excessive drinking?" A clearly uncomfortable Eldridge could only say that "no medical man could answer that and I'm sure I can't." Who can say how much truth there was to Welch's claims and insinuations, but he had certainly accomplished his goal of portraying Lind as not only a wife-stealer but also a drunk.

On May 18, the trial was disrupted in a mysterious way, as Justice Moore ordered witness Lamar Johnson to come to his chambers. Following a twenty-minute discussion, Johnson exited, and Moore conferred with the lawyers from both sides. Moore then announced that the jury would be sequestered for the remainder of the trial. Only later would the full story emerge. Truck driver Walter Lee Yow, thirty-six, of High Point, North Carolina, had called defense lawyer Welch and told quite a story. He claimed that he was driving a load back from Brooklyn, New York, and stopped at the trial because he was interested in the case. While taking a bathroom break in the court building, Johnson approached him and offered him $100 to take the stand and corroborate his story that Miller placed the envelope in the car. Johnson denied the story, and investigation quickly showed that Yow had been arrested thirty-seven times and forcibly given mental examinations twice to determine if he was sane. Conferring with Judge Moore, Yow admitted that he had been recently detained by authorities in Lynchburg, Virginia, because they thought "I was a wild man" and in another jurisdiction "because people thought I was a little cranky." It was soon apparent that Yow's story was a flight of fancy, and in July, he received a one-year sentence on an obstruction of justice charge.

Marguerite Miller was of course one of the most highly anticipated witnesses. She was excluded from attending the first week of the trial so she wouldn't hear the testimony of other witnesses. When she did get on the stand, everything she said was in support of her husband and his self-defense story. She claimed that she knew the envelope on the seat held a gun, as she saw it every time she went into Lind's car, and she stated positively that on the fatal day, "I observed the gun on the seat when I opened the door." When asked by the prosecution how long Lind had the gun in the car, all she could say was, "No definite time," and when pressed for a specific answer, she said that it was for a few years. She then went one better and claimed that Lind did reach for the gun as he saw Miller approach the car despite her telling him not to. Underscoring her point, she added that Lind announced, "I'll shoot that old gray-haired bastard's head off" as he prepared to use the weapon. She also took pains to refute a story that when dining with Lind and his son in December 1943, she warned her lover to watch out because "Bob says he's going to kill you." She was firmly sticking with the story that Lind was the one making threats against her husband and there was no premeditation from Robert Miller.

She added some juicy details about her relationship with Dr. Lind, with none of the stories designed to make him look good. According to

A worried-looking Marguerite Miller clings to a member of her husband's defense team while wearing the same coat she wore the day of Lind's murder. *Courtesy of AP Wirephoto.*

Marguerite, over their five-year relationship, she gave him a total of $5,000 for various bills and car payments; in fact, she helped pay for the car he died in. The defense brought a series of business owners to testify to various bills Marguerite paid for Lind, ranging from weekly $20 to $25 grocery bills to a car radio and defroster. She had even cashed out an insurance policy to give him money, and she cryptically but insinuatingly said she couldn't recall if that was the time he got into trouble with another woman or whether Dr. Overholser (Lind's boss) "got after him." She elaborated that she had given Lind money to pay a woman who had been waiting decades to marry him, presumably to prevent a breach of promise case. She added that Lind was always "very hard up" because there were always judgments against him in court. Marguerite claimed that she kept up the payments because Lind blackmailed her and threatened to reveal their relationship to her husband. She had plenty of denials, too: she never wanted to divorce her husband, never had a key to Lind's house and never said she wanted to move in with him. This was in response to testimony from Lind's daughter that there had been discussion of her and her two children moving in with Lind while her husband was away in the army. Marguerite had wanted to move in herself and argued against the proposal, leading to resentment between her and Lind's family. Like so much in the case, the jury would simply have to decide who to believe.

Marguerite Miller's niece and namesake Marguerite Fien also aided the defense's case in her testimony. She told a vivid story of how Lind and her aunt came to her house in September 1943. Marguerite Miller looked upset and worried and was scared that a flashing light outside was from her husband's car. Lind boasted that he wasn't nervous about Miller following them and took a pistol from his pocket, allegedly saying, "I expect to see and shoot him first. I feel far more capable of handling a gun than Bob Miller. If anyone gets killed it won't be me." This was followed by a period of time when Lind would supposedly call Fien two or three times a week to inquire about Miller's health problems and gloat with statements like, "I hope it's nothing trivial. I hope he dies. I'm no hypocrite. I hope we have a good time dancing on his grave." (Why he wouldn't have just asked his mistress about her husband's health was left conveniently unanswered by Fien.) Fien's husband, Edward, backed up her story, commenting that he remembered Lind showing off his gun and threatening Miller's life, dryly noting that "that doesn't happen out at my house every time I have guests." Despite this, Prosecutor Maher noted that Fien and her family's stories seemed too specific and too well-rehearsed to be fully authentic, sounding like "the same regular monotony of a phonograph with a stuck needle."

But the most anticipated witness of all was Robert Miller himself. (Although she had attended the trial every day since testifying, his wife discreetly was not present for his testimony.) Miller reiterated what his attorneys had argued over the past two weeks. He sobbed while testifying about the affair, saying he learned about it in July 1943 when he picked up an extension phone and heard the two conversing lovingly. Asked to describe how he felt about the discovery, he was unable to reply for a full three minutes as he sobbed and then finally replied that "it crucified me." He confronted his wife almost daily about the affair, and she promised to end it several times but never did.

At other times she would "get mad, curse me, and throw things at me" if he brought up the subject. Moreover, he testified that he had feared for his life for months. According to him, he asked Lind three times to stop seeing his wife, to no avail. Several months before the shooting, he confronted Lind when he was in court as an expert witness and told him to leave his wife alone. Miller added that he would go to Lind's boss, Dr. Winfred Overholser, if he didn't break off the affair. Lind responded with a thinly veiled threat on his life and told him to "go to hell," but Miller didn't want any "notoriety," so he didn't go through with his threat to approach Overholser. Presumably, that's why he also did not go to the police. He added that the Fien family relayed Lind's threats toward him as well. At his wit's end, all he could do was pray for guidance and began to light holy candles in his darkened law office and spend hours thinking and praying in silence.

In Miller's telling, on February 21 he went to the store to meet his wife and simply tried to prevent her from meeting with Lind. After looking in the store and not seeing her (despite having initially claimed he was never in the store at all), he spotted her getting into Lind's car, and he claimed that he only told her to leave when he reached into the car. Lind then threatened him, and he saw Lind's hand go downward like he was reaching for a gun, and his mind went rather conveniently blank. He also claimed that he didn't remember meeting attorney Harn on the streetcar, leading prosecutor Murray to ask why he could remember some things before the shooting and not others. Miller could only say, "I can't explain it."

Having done their best to prove that Miller acted under threat from Lind, the defense team attempted to also prove that their client was mentally unstable at the time. Welch said he would prove that Miller was of unsound mind but made sure to note that "a man of unsound mind can shoot in self-defense." Essentially, if the jury didn't buy the self-defense argument, Miller still wasn't responsible for his actions due to his mental state. (Although how a man was sufficiently mentally unstable to not be responsible for his actions yet mentally stable enough to have a lightning-quick reaction to perceived danger was never quite explained by Welch or his associates.) A parade of twenty-one character witnesses prominent in Washington society and government testified that after finding out about the affair, Miller changed from a jovial and gentlemanly fellow to a mentally unhinged one who had shed forty pounds through worry and stress. Several confirmed Miller's testimony that he would spend hours every day praying and staring at holy candles in his office with the lights off. His behavior became so concerning that another lawyer and an insurance agent from an adjoining office agreed to always stay with Miller over lunch so he wouldn't be unobserved. Another longtime friend said he started to avoid Miller because he constantly talked about his cheating wife and sounds in his head that he described "like a train stopping." U.S. Marshal John Colpoys made a reference to "Bob Miller, as we knew him affectionately," which drew an objection from Murray. In the most bizarre moment, first assistant U.S. attorney John Fihelly, chief of the criminal division of the U.S. attorney's office, testified on Miller's behalf. Thus, the boss of prosecutors Murray and Maher was in effect testifying for the opposing side! Fihelly testified that Miller twice sought advice for him about his marriage problems, and he was the one who advised him to talk to Lind and then threaten to go to Overholser. Fihelly stated that he knew Miller for twenty-five years and said he was previously "superoptimistic" and "immaculate in appearance" but changed in the last eight to ten months and would look distracted, unkempt and unshaven. Not surprisingly, Murray declined to cross-examine his boss.

There was a predictable disconnect between psychiatry experts called by the defense and those called by the prosecution. Using the same tactic that appeared in William Reaguer's trial, the defense offered a thirty-four-minute-long hypothetical question that described Miller as a man not in control of his mental faculties. Dr. Harry Crawford testified for the defense and said that for twenty-five minutes before the shooting, Miller's actions were "automatic and on the vegetative level" and he was incapable of forming premeditation. Asked by prosecutors what condition Miller supposedly had, Crawford said he couldn't give a name to it and that it "was a temporary mental upset. There is no categorical name for it." This temporary condition was then followed by a memory lock that began after the "peak of the confusional moment." Dr. Albert Marland was also called by the defense and gave similar testimony, adding that if a lawyer of Miller's experience did plant the gun in Lind's car, it would have been "a rather foolish thing for a man of his experience to do." The defense's third expert witness, Dr. Antoine Schneider, went further and said that if Miller placed the gun in the car, he was either mentally unsound or "unbelievably stupid." The reader may recognize Dr. Schneider as the man who testified to Reaguer's "hardened arteries made him do it" defense and will be happy to know that he still subscribed to the same theory. Schneider noted that based on two examinations of Miller, he found him to be suffering from "an arteriosclerotic condition of the vessels of the brain" that was a secondary cause to the mental strain caused by his wife's affair. Schneider decided Miller was "suffering from one of the lesser mental disturbances—a psycho-neurosis of the type in which anxiety is predominant," although prosecutor Murray got him to acknowledge that it is difficult to tell true amnesia from fake amnesia. Schneider added that Miller's behavior was abnormal because he was constantly asking for advice about his affair when he normally gave it in his profession and that the "ultra-religious fixation" he developed was too extreme to be normal. The government called expert witnesses of their own, and there were few surprises in their testimony. Dr. Jacob Conn and Dr. Robert Seliger looked at the same information as the defense witnesses and stated the opposite conclusion, that Miller was sane at the time of the murder. Dr. Conn added that his answer would not change whether or not Miller placed the gun in the car; in other words, with or without premeditation, he was sane.

In his three-and-a-half-hour closing plea on May 30, Welch quoted from Fihelly's testimony when he looked toward Miller and said, "Keep your chin up, Bob. You'll come out all right." Welch melodramatically added that while the jury was deliberating, Miller's "torn and bleeding heart stays here in the courtroom and prays for deliverance and relief from the agony of mind and the torture of soul which an unfaithful woman and a sinful man have heaped upon him." He unloaded on both Lind and Marguerite Miller, saying that Lind was a "sadist" and a "half-drunk, lecherous housebreaker" who "used his God-given talents strictly and solely as tools of the devil....He knew more how to seduce a woman than any other creature walking on God's green earth." For her part, Welch referred to Marguerite as a "lying, double-dealing woman who broke the heart of a home-loving husband." Murray and Maher must have known that they could not create the same amount of sympathy for the deceased Dr. Lind, and in their closing arguments, they reiterated the logic of their case for premeditation. Marguerite Miller didn't escape lacerating words from them either, as Maher said she was "as versatile in changing her stories as she is in changing her affections....We have seen that she can change her affections in a flash—to be specific, two flashes—the flashes of two pistol shots." It was a good point; as soon as her lover was dead, she seems to have very quickly returned her affections to her husband, standing 100 percent behind his account even if some of her stories seemed rather creaky. Besides all of the testimony they had heard, the members of the jury were also shown Lind's car and a map of the crime scene, although they never went there in person. Following the closing arguments, the attorneys conferred with Justice Moore about jury instructions.

Moore delivered his instructions to the jury on the afternoon of the thirty-first, telling jurors that they should consider the claim of self-defense first. If they did not agree to acquit Miller on that point, they should then consider

A pleased Robert Miller (*center, in dark suit*) stands alongside his defense team following his acquittal. *Courtesy of AP Wirephoto.*

the insanity claim. Miller's political friends stood by him throughout the trial, and as the jury retired, former senator Thomas Gore told Miller, "We'll go to the races again together, Bob, when this thing is all over." The jury was not gone long; deliberations began at 5:21 p.m., and the jury foreman sent word at 6:25 p.m. that they were ready to deliver their verdict. In the courtroom, it was announced: not guilty. Jurors later revealed to the press that there was no debate at all. They actually agreed on the verdict during the first ballot, but as one juror said, "it would look better if we waited a little while," so they made small talk for an hour!

As his eighty-year-old brother Fred embraced him, Miller simply offered a "thank you" to those involved in the trial, particularly his defense team and Judge Moore, but as he left, he curtly refused to ride in the same elevator as prosecutors Murray and Maher. Taking the next prosecutor-free elevator, he walked across the street to his law office, a free man. Marguerite was waiting for him there and, as he arrived, shouted, "Lordy, Lordy…Bob, Bob!" Miller was back in court on June 2 as if nothing had ever interrupted his law practice; he won the larceny case he was representing. For the most part, he avoided the press, but he did tell a reporter that within days of his acquittal he received two large mail bags full of congratulatory letters from across the country. Unspoken sentiment in favor of the "unwritten law" may well have determined the verdict regardless of what the lawyers said. Miller probably also did benefit from his many associations with the Washington legal and political world. Thus, even though some of the key issues like the fingerprints on the envelope or Lind's supposed ownership of the gun were never actually resolved, the primary issue was likely never in doubt, despite its drama. Robert Miller lived until 1963 and his wife until 1965; as of the 1950 census, they were still married. Whether it is significant that he is buried next to his first wife rather than his second is left to the reader's interpretation.

CHAPTER 4

IN THE CATHEDRAL'S SHADOW

Murder can strike anywhere, but in 1944, Washington, D.C., experienced a violent death in a particularly unexpected location. Washington National Cathedral—or, more properly speaking, the Cathedral Church of Saint Peter and Saint Paul in the City and Diocese of Washington—rose above Northwest D.C. starting in the early 1900s. The huge Episcopal cathedral was still being worked on in 1944 (and would be for decades after World War II), although wartime building restrictions had slowed construction. Yet it was still an impressive building in 1944, and several other buildings were also on the campus. Most relevant to our story, the Cathedral had a library building just forty yards to the east of the main building. The library was a gift from Violet Blair Janin in memory of her mother, Mary Jesup Blair. It opened in 1927 and included five thousand of Janin's personal books among its collection of thirty-six thousand volumes on theology and church history.

The library had experienced a bit of scandal in April 1937 when Adrienne Courtenay, twenty-seven, and Dorothy Lawrence, twenty-eight, were found dead in their shared gas-filled apartment by their landlord, lying under a blanket in bed "clasped in each other's arms." Papers of the time could only hint at the obvious nature of the women's relationship, noting that in a lengthy suicide note the two requested to be cremated and have their ashes mixed together (with the request promptly denied by their families). Courtenay had worked at the library as its secretary up until two months or so before the dual suicide, and papers did not hesitate to

Washington's National Cathedral was still undergoing construction work in 1944. *Courtesy of AP Wirephoto.*

mention this fact. Needless to say, a lesbian suicide pact was not the sort of press the library wanted.

Courtenay still worked at the library when a new assistant librarian joined the staff in 1936. Catherine Cooper Reardon, thirty-seven years old in 1944, was born in Alexandria, Virginia, and educated at the Hannah More Academy in Reisterstown, Maryland, before attending William and Mary. Through the years, she also spent several summers at the University of Virginia and Middlebury College in Vermont taking additional classes. From 1928 to 1932, she taught French and Latin at Blackstone High School in rural southern Virginia. Four years in Southside Virginia was evidently enough for her, and in 1932, she became an assistant librarian at St. John's College in Annapolis, Maryland. She worked there through 1935 and in 1936 came to D.C. to assume a similar position at the National Cathedral's library, although it was noted that a head librarian was never hired, so in effect she was the chief librarian. One can't help but assume that the Cathedral was trying to save some payroll money with that maneuver. She

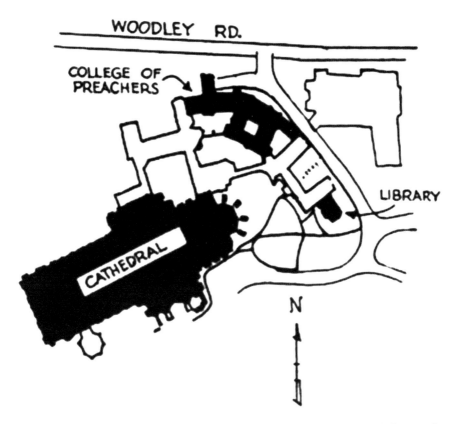

This map shows the location of the library building in relation to the Cathedral. *Courtesy of Washington Evening Star.*

was hired by the Very Reverend ZeBarney Phillips (yes, ZeBarney was really his given name), dean of the cathedral, rector at the parish church that Reardon attended and chaplain of the Senate. The two enjoyed what papers called a "deep spiritual kinship," and when he died in 1942, a coworker said that Reardon was "crushed and acted as though suffering a personal loss." To our more cynical twenty-first-century minds, there are a couple of newspaper descriptions of their relationship that seem to hint at more than just a friendship, but this was probably not intended by the writers at the time.

Reardon's father died when she was a young child, and she remained very close with her mother, Lulie, throughout her life. When she accepted the job in D.C., she moved in with her mother, residing at 3715 Woodley Road NW, just a five-minute walk from the library. Acquaintances reported that she "worried constantly" over her mother's ill health and had recently been to the doctor several times herself with health concerns. Lulie apparently was ill enough that she had been bedridden for a year. Even for someone who worked in a religious library, Catherine was viewed by those who knew her as a "spiritual type" who frequently read religious books and would periodically take a break from working throughout the day to kneel in prayer at one of the Cathedral's chapels. She was variously described as "attractive" and "comely" in papers and called "quiet, sensitive, and introspective" by one acquaintance; a coworker said she was a "quiet, conscientious person who didn't mix much." It was also said by those who

Catherine Cooper Reardon as she appeared upon her graduation from William and Mary. *Courtesy of the* College of William & Mary Colonial Echo.

knew her that she was a "sweet and lovely" person who apparently just liked to be alone. She was known to spend hours sitting in the Bishop's Garden at the Cathedral, admiring the flowers, and she "found joy" arranging flowers at her parish church. On the rare occasions when she did go out, it was with her mother or aunt Corinne. While most accounts portrayed her as content in her solitude, neighbor Alberta O'Connell offered a different perspective. She told the media that Reardon often told her that she disliked working by herself in the lonely "crypt," as she called her basement work area. One acquaintance claimed that she had once referred to herself as "a poor fish," a reference to her Pisces sign, and another said that she was interested in astrology and metaphysics.

On the evening of March 1, 1944, Lulie Reardon became concerned as the hours went by without Catherine putting in an appearance at their shared apartment. Press reports initially carried conflicting and confusingly different accounts ascribed to Lulie Reardon, variously stating when Catherine was last seen. In one newspaper article, Lulie was quoted as saying that Catherine came home for lunch that day and then went back to work. By another account, Catherine came home from work at 5:00 p.m. and then said that she was going to the grocery store to get dinner. Yet another suggested that Catherine hadn't been seen by her mother all day and she simply assumed that her daughter had gone to the grocery store after work.

Later accounts tended to agree that this last timeline was the correct one; the other accounts likely conflated Catherine's activities from the day before with those on March 1. Regardless of the last time Catherine was seen, her mother noticed that Catherine had been in a "despondent mood," no doubt only increasing her anxiety when Catherine hadn't returned home by 7:00 p.m. At 9:30 p.m., Lulie notified Corinne Reardon, Catherine's aunt, that she was missing. At 1:15 a.m., Corinne notified the police, although not much seems to have been done by them. Lulie also called Helen Young, the library's archivist, who apparently was also a neighbor. Young came to the Reardon apartment and found the older woman so upset that she spent the night with her.

By now, Young was worried as well, and on the morning of March 2, she called the library's curator, John Bayless, and told him that Reardon had never returned home. This worried Bayless, for the day before he had seen Reardon sitting on the library steps and crying, but she wouldn't tell him what was wrong. Lending weight to the acquaintance's statements about Reardon's depression, Bayless's first impression was that she had killed herself, a rather odd conclusion unless Reardon had a history of appearing depressed. Although not scheduled to work that day, he told Young that he would meet her at the library and they would see if Reardon was there. Upon reaching the building, Bayless and Young noted that the door to the library was locked. They soon became thoroughly perplexed; the ever-reliable and predictable Catherine Reardon wasn't there to meet them. Looking around the main rooms of the library, they found no sign of her but were even more puzzled when they found her coat, gloves and purse on a chair. This wasn't unusual in itself, for Reardon typically left these items in this spot; the mystery was that Reardon should have been close by. Just after 9:00 a.m., they descended into the basement level, which was where Reardon worked most of the time at her desk and where the library's most valuable books were kept. They had looked for her there earlier, but now they would search more thoroughly. Bayless noticed that the bathroom door near Reardon's desk was open. He looked inside and was shocked to see bloodstains on the floor; it was clear that someone had tried to wipe up a considerable amount of blood. More bloodstains would later be found on nearby bookstacks. Looking around, his attention was grabbed by a small door that he had never taken notice of before. Something instinctively told him he needed to investigate it, and he saw more traces of blood near the door. He opened the little door and ducked inside and then saw that a small iron ladder led down about five feet to a subbasement utility room holding the building's steam

Left: The library building where Reardon worked and met her death. The arrow points to the subbasement where her body was found. *Courtesy of AP Wirephoto.*

Opposite: An understandably stunned-looking Helen Young, Reardon's coworker, leaves the library building following the discovery of the body. *Courtesy of AP Wirephoto.*

pipes. He climbed down into the darkened space, didn't see anything and was about to leave when he noticed a "small partitioned space" about six feet by eight feet in size on one side of the subbasement. Peering into what he called an "aperture," he recoiled in horror when he saw a woman's body filling up the space. He had found Catherine Reardon.

Bayless immediately called the police, but bizarrely, the police were already on their way. Someone had called the Metropolitan Police that morning and informed them that "a young woman has been murdered in Washington Cathedral. You fellows had better get busy." The caller then hung up, and the police dispatched officers to investigate the report. Investigators later insisted that the mystery call came in before the one made by Bayless. Police concluded that the call was made by a "heckler" who had somehow found out about the murder before Bayless called rather than the killer. It was a mystery that was never really resolved, although it is perhaps somewhat less mysterious than it sounds. Maybe other Cathedral employees heard word about the body's discovery very quickly and someone placed a call, or perhaps it was indeed the person who had placed her in the isolated spot.

Regardless of who first notified them, by 10:20 a.m., police had arrived at the crime scene. As police officers approached the body, they saw a blood-soaked men's undershirt lying near it. There was an obvious wound to Reardon's head and a small laceration on her throat. Officers presumed her head had been "smashed by a pipe or similar instrument." Looking at the body, detectives thought they were dealing with a sex crime, as it appeared that Reardon was clad only in her slip and brassiere. Initial

newspaper reports stated this as a fact, but later a detective said that she was "fully clothed except for an undergarment." There was never any dispute that her panties had been removed and then tossed in with the body. There is probably a simple explanation for the apparent discrepancy over whether her dress was removed. Reports of the crime scene note that her dress was bunched up under her head and shoulders. It had probably not been removed but rather accidentally pulled up around her shoulders as she was manhandled and shoved into the narrow space. Looking at the body *in situ*, it looked like the dress had been removed and placed under her head, although this was not the case. Incongruously, Reardon's shoes were neatly set beside her body.

After conferring with Young, Bayless and James Berkeley, the Cathedral's verger (a layperson who assists with various organizational or caretaking duties in a church), detectives soon realized who they wanted to talk to. While the perceived sexual element remained initially murky, Chief of Detectives Robert Barrett quickly theorized that it was a revenge killing because Reardon had complained to Berkeley several days before that the library's janitor and handyman, a Black man named Julius Fisher, was "shirking his job." Suspiciously, Fisher did not show up to work on March 2. Barrett later told reporters that he knew Fisher's identity within twenty-five minutes of arriving at the crime scene. Detectives quickly began looking for Fisher and received information about some of his "known haunts," not just in D.C. but also in Vienna and Alexandria, Virginia, and Baltimore. Detective Sergeant Edgar Scott and another officer went to Fisher's home at 4806 Hayes Street NE. Fisher was not home, nor was his wife, Elizabeth, whom he had married in September 1942. In an act that would make any modern-day jurist cringe, Scott and his partner entered the house and began looking around. They hit paydirt in a bedroom closet; inside they found "blood-soaked trousers, [a] sweater and shoes" shoved into the back of the closet, along with a pocketknife. (No legal issue was ever made regarding the nature of the search.) An FBI specialist later confirmed following testing that the bloodstains on the clothes were human.

Scott and his partner then went to one of the places they had been tipped off about, a restaurant at 18th Street and U Street NW. Sure enough, thirty-four-year-old Julius Fisher was sitting in the restaurant, eating a sandwich and drinking beer and whiskey. Scott and the other officer walked up to Fisher and told him they wanted to ask him some questions about "a felony that was committed the other day." Without saying anything else, Fisher gulped down a shot of whiskey, grabbed his sandwich and told the officers, "Let's get going." The trio entered the police car, and while the two detectives later claimed to have frisked Fisher, they almost ruined their impressive capture. On the drive to police headquarters, Scott noticed that Fisher was holding his hat over his right hand, so he pushed the hat aside and was surprised to see that Fisher was holding a .32-caliber revolver. Scott grabbed the weapon and angrily asked Fisher, using racially loaded language, "What

A reporter rather nervously looks into the subbasement where Reardon's body was found. *Courtesy of AP Wirephoto.*

did you want to do, boy, kill a couple of policemen?" Fisher hung his head and answered, "No, I wanted to shoot myself." Once at police headquarters, detectives asked Fisher questions for about fifteen minutes, and then Scott dramatically brought out the bloody pants and shirt he had found in Fisher's closet and placed them in front of the man. Fisher thought for a moment and

Reardon's body is removed from the library building. *Courtesy of AP Wirephoto.*

quietly said that there was blood on the clothes because "I had some trouble with the lady at the Cathedral library." Fisher then "freely admitted the crime" and told detectives "all the details." As he talked, police transcribed his confession and had him sign it. Fisher also traveled with them back to his house, telling them that they had missed a piece of evidence. He showed them where he had hidden Reardon's William and Mary garnet class ring.

A coroner's jury was immediately scheduled, but Fisher clammed up and declined to testify. He sat through the inquest without apparent emotion, staring straight ahead and asking no questions. Deputy Coroner Christopher Murphy provided more details on the nature of Reardon's death. He testified that death was caused in two possible ways. A blow to the head from a heavy object that fractured the skull from front to back "like an egg shell" was potentially fatal. A second fracture occurred when Reardon fell and hit the floor. There was also evidence of strangulation, and Murphy summarized that the cause of death was "asphyxiation caused by strangulation, and a fractured skull…either one would have killed her." Additionally, there was a small cut on Reardon's throat, but it couldn't have been fatal since it barely pierced the skin. There were also several bruises and abrasions on her body, but nothing major. Murphy placed the time of death at about 6:00 p.m. on March 1. Death was probably not instant but occurred soon after the blow to the head. Murphy did not add any clarity as to whether there was a sexual motive to the crime, as he testified that he was "not ready to say" that she had been raped "but indicated it was possible and investigations were continuing."

While the legal wheels began turning, a short prayer service was held in the church office on March 2, and a more elaborate memorial service was held on the morning of March 4 in the Cathedral's Bethlehem Chapel. Although initially prostrated with grief, Reardon's mother and several other family members attended the service. After the memorial service, a further funeral service was held at the home of Catherine's grandmother in Alexandria, attended by over two hundred people; papers noted that 80 percent of the attendees were female. Interment followed in Alexandria's Presbyterian Cemetery. (Mother Lulie Reardon died just under eight months later, and one can suppose what effect her daughter's passing had on her health.)

A grand jury swiftly convened, and a newspaper article noted that the grand jury acted with "unusual speed" and indicted Fisher for first-degree murder on March 5. In fact, the grand jury took all of fourteen minutes to make its decision. Washington's newspaper for the Black community, the *Washington Afro American*, offered a perspective not found in other papers when a reporter spoke to Fisher's wife, Elizabeth. It's unclear how much she knew about the evidence offered at the inquest, but she told the reporter that "I don't believe he did it" and noted that his mother and several siblings also lived in D.C. Arraignment was delayed slightly to allow for Fisher to meet with his attorney, who was en route from Detroit, but the arraignment followed on March 17. Six counts were filed, with three dealing with the various ways Reardon was injured: choking and strangling, causing the skull fracture and causing her to hit her head against an object, resulting in the second fracture. The other charges essentially repeated the first three with the addition that the injuries were caused while in the act of robbery, based on the theft of her class ring. By the time of the trial, the robbery counts would be dropped and the charges consolidated down to two: murder by choking or strangulation and murder by bludgeoning. The fact that no rape charge was filed seems to speak for itself, but the issue of a possible sexual motive would briefly arise at trial. At the arraignment, Fisher pleaded not guilty. Fisher did testify at the grand jury hearing, and while more information became available to the public, the full story that Fisher had to tell would only emerge at trial.

Amid the issues that eventually emerged at trial, one discrepancy that curiously didn't seem to attract much attention was the time of Reardon's death. It should be said that the trial transcript has evidently not survived, so only excerpts of trial testimony survive in other court documents. Perhaps this and other unclear points were ironed out in the missing trial transcript. From what records are available, Fisher initially placed the time of her death at around 9:00 a.m., and this is what the police publicly reported. Later, Fisher stated that he killed Reardon at about noon, with no reason given for the change in testimony, and this is the time that seems to show up most often in surviving court documents. Recall that press reports had conflicting stories about when Reardon was last seen, and a 9:00 a.m. or noon time of death fits with the timeline that she wasn't seen at home all day. Reardon's reported death time of 6:00 p.m., per the autopsy, jived more with the earlier accounts attributed to Lulie Reardon, but estimated death times are always an inexact science. At least one newspaper article explicitly accepted the noon time of death and stated that Murphy's estimate was off. Coworkers reported that it would have been unusual for Reardon to be there at 5:00 or 6:00 p.m. and noted that employees did not have to complete a timecard or check in with a supervisor; they worked "on their honor." Fisher's normal work schedule was reportedly 7:00 a.m. to 3:00 p.m., so he would not likely be there at 5:00 or 6:00 p.m. either. All of this shows that even in a case where there is no doubt about who the killer is, not all of the threads come together, particularly in historical cases where not all of the records survive. In the end, the time of Reardon's death doesn't particularly change anything significant about the nature of Fisher's guilt.

U.S. attorney Edward Curran led the prosecution case, assisted by Charles Murray, fresh off the unsuccessful prosecution of Robert Miller. Justice

Charles Houston made his best effort to save Julius Fisher's life while also trying to address racial inequalities. *Courtesy of the Library of Congress.*

James Proctor presided over the trial. Fisher had acquired a rather notable defense lawyer, Charles Houston, perhaps the most famous Black lawyer in the country and the general counsel for the NAACP. Houston mentored famous figures like Thurgood Marshall and likely would be better known today except for his rather early death in 1950. Julius Fisher would not suffer from lack of effective counsel. Eight women and four men were selected for the jury, a somewhat unusual balance for cases of the period, but clearly the prosecution felt that women would be more likely to convict someone for the murder of another female. Given that it was 1944, the occupations of all eight women were unsurprisingly listed in papers as "housewife," while the men's professions included real estate salesman, truck driver, train clerk and office manager. The defense exhausted all twenty challenges, but the prosecution felt the need to use only two. Not surprisingly, there were no Black members of the jury, and Justice Proctor "closely inquired whether any racial prejudice would influence" each prospective juror. Race was an inescapable subtext of the entire case from the beginning.

There was never any dispute over Fisher's guilt; Houston was only trying to save Fisher's life by arguing that there was no premeditation involved and that the "slain woman's personality caused the accused man to fly into a rage." He would greatly elaborate on that theory during the trial. Because of the overwhelming evidence of Fisher's guilt, Houston couldn't have Fisher renounce his confession entirely and proclaim his innocence, but if the confession was not admitted as evidence, jurors would have only Fisher's trial testimony to consider. As we will see, this later trial testimony presumably had been shaped to portray events more favorably than in the confession. The prosecution quickly introduced Fisher's confession from the night of his arrest into evidence over "strenuous defense objections."

Houston argued that Fisher hadn't been sufficiently informed of his rights before giving his confession. According to Fisher, once taken into custody, he was punched in the mouth and kicked in the side by detectives, and he was never informed about his constitutional rights. Houston also questioned the accuracy of the confession as a literal transcript, noting that police officers said they spent one hour and twenty-five minutes getting it, yet it only took twelve minutes for an officer to read it out loud in court. Several officers were brought to the stand to rebut Fisher's version of events, and they insisted that there was no violence inflicted on him. However, Detective Sergeant Scott, while denying that Fisher was "mistreated," admitted that he hadn't read him his "constitutional rights and [told him] that everything he said would be used against him." But by the standards of 1944, Fisher was evidently told enough that the confession was never thrown out.

From the beginning of the case, investigators knew that Reardon had made some sort of complaint about Fisher's work performance, and this is apparently what sparked the murderous event. Fisher said that the week before the murder, Reardon complained to verger James Berkeley that Fisher had not dusted under her desk in the basement level of the library. Berkeley had hired Fisher just before Christmas at a salary of $110 a month and had not heard any other complaints about him. Little else was said in the press about Fisher's background other than for one paper to note the dark irony that Washington city directories previously listed him as an exterminator, among other menial jobs. Berkeley described him as a "quiet, unassuming fellow—not a tough character," a characterization supported by all other witnesses. Fisher was responsible for cleaning three buildings and doing odd jobs; he carried a set of keys to the library building. He later said that he enjoyed his job and liked not having to report to someone throughout the day. Following Reardon's complaint, Berkeley spoke to Fisher about that matter and "mildly reprimanded" him, but Berkeley didn't feel like Fisher bore any resentment for what seemed to be a minor matter. He elaborated that Fisher's reaction was "[j]ust the usual thing—what you'd expect from anyone. He said he would be more careful." In fact, on the stand Fisher claimed that he didn't resent Reardon's earlier complaint and hadn't thought about it, although as we shall see, his confession rather contradicted this claim. Houston wanted to convince the jury that Fisher hadn't brooded over the complaint, or else it would appear that Fisher was acting out of premeditation to settle a grudge. To set up this argument, Houston said he would show what "disposition" Reardon had. Fisher said that Berkeley described Reardon as "half-cracked" at one point, and when Berkeley took the stand, Houston asked him if, when he reprimanded Fisher, he said, "Don't say anything about it to Miss Reardon. She's a little cracked!" Berkeley denied using that exact phrase but admitted that "I told him that Miss Reardon was peculiar or odd in some ways." Hence, Houston was trying to show that Berkeley had made clear to Fisher that he understood that Reardon was blowing things out of proportion and Fisher shouldn't be troubled by the complaint. Houston made an interesting point later in the trial to support this idea when he asked Detective Scott whether Fisher's house was "neat and clean" when he searched it. Scott confirmed that it was, and Houston was clearly trying to show that Reardon was irrational when it came to Fisher's cleaning habits and presumably irrational in general. Houston's reason for not pursuing the theory that Fisher acted in revenge will soon become more apparent, as he had another line of defense that he wanted to focus on.

The jury took a bus to the crime scene early in the trial and examined the building all the way from the attic to the subbasement where the body was found. Distances were measured for various points related to the crime, down to the detail of noting that there were twenty-one steps in the spiral staircase leading to the murder scene. During the library visit, reporters watched as the normally "impassive" Fisher "lost his composure briefly at the library." When leaving, Fisher "broke into a run when photographers attempted to snap his picture, half-dragging the handcuffed marshal along with him." Once in a police car, he hid his face in his hands; throughout the remainder of the trial, Fisher would show no emotion. After returning from the visit to the crime scene, prosecutors referred to locations they had seen that contained spatters of Reardon's blood, including book stacks and two desks.

Prosecutors then described the confession Fisher gave on the night of his arrest and asked Fisher to clarify or elaborate on certain points. Between his confession and courtroom testimony, Fisher gave somewhat different versions of how the fatal events occurred. In both versions, he said he was cleaning in the basement when Reardon came downstairs. The critical difference between his stories was who initiated the conversation that followed. In his confession, he stated that he asked her why she had complained about his work and declared, "You know I keep the place clean." She responded, "Well, if you cleaned this place up all right, what is this dust doing under my desk?" In court, he claimed that he passed Reardon on a set of stairs that morning without saying anything. Seeing her a few minutes later, she started the exchange by asking if he had dusted, to which he replied, "Certainly, doesn't it look like it? I always try to keep it clean." She then told him that's what he was paid to do, and he asked if she was trying to get him in trouble. Clearly, the first version supported a view of premeditation since he was the one to start the conversation. Recall his claim that he hadn't thought about her complaint and didn't resent it, but if he cared enough to confront her about it, that clearly wasn't the case. Regardless of which telling was true, in both a critical element of his story was what Reardon said next. In his confession, he initially said that she "called me a name—a name no white person ever called me before." In court, he made explicit what was already quite obvious, and the reader must be warned that strong racial language follows. On the stand, Fisher claimed that "she called me a black n----r. No white person had ever called me a 'n----r' before. I had been called that by my own colored people." This sent him into an uncontrollable rage. As he told it:

> Something rose in my chest....I got angry and smacked her. It looked like I got angry inside and it welled up in my chest. She screamed and ran to the back of the office. The screams got on my nerves and I got scared and nervous—the screams were so loud. So I ran upstairs, grabbed a stick, and hit her with it....She started squawking...The stick broke, so I choked her and she seemed to become unconscious. Then I dragged her out. I wasn't trying to kill her but trying to stop her from making the noise. She squawked again while I was wiping up the blood. I choked her but there was no noise, so I stabbed her. She stopped then.

Houston made the racial slur a key part of his defense against premeditation: Fisher didn't intend to harm Reardon until she said that. Of course, the problem was that there was only Fisher's word that it ever happened. There doesn't seem to have been any testimony exploring whether Reardon had been known to use that slur before. Intriguingly, one newspaper article referenced an acquaintance of Reardon's who claimed that the librarian had complained about the janitor being introduced to her as "Mr. Fisher," granting him a level of respect she apparently didn't think he deserved. The paper ascribed this to the fact that Reardon was of a "southern background," but whatever racial prejudices she really held remain murky.

The prosecution tried to counter the defense gambit by pointing to Fisher's confession, where he said that he told Reardon after slapping her, "If I don't kill you, it will be the end of me," which Fisher later denied saying. Even if Fisher was thrown into a rage by a racial slur, the prosecution wanted to make clear that he was still acting deliberately and thoughtfully. The "stick" Fisher grabbed was in fact a twenty-nine-inch piece of firewood from the fireplace in the upstairs reading room. He struck Reardon hard enough that it broke into several pieces, and after the murder, he deposited the pieces back into the fireplace, trying to hide the evidence. Detectives hadn't thought to look through the fireplace as they first investigated the scene, and newsmen traipsed through the reading room all day, not knowing they were standing right next to the murder weapon. Only after Fisher's confession did detectives go and collect the broken pieces of firewood. At trial, Special Investigator David Ennis testified how he pieced together four large bloodstained pieces and four smaller splinters like a puzzle, and the makeshift weapon was shown to the jury.

Fisher clarified in court that it was actually after he had dragged and carried Reardon down to the subbasement that he noticed that she "was still making moaning noises, so I went down there and stuck a knife in her throat to make her keep quiet." He then "pulled off her panties" to clean up the blood on the floor. Recall that while early reports stated that her dress had been removed, this had turned out to not be the case. Deputy Coroner Murphy returned to the stand during the trial and stated that there was no evidence of sexual assault. While one would think the prosecution would still want to suggest some sort of sexual motive, interestingly, they did not pursue that route. When Houston asked Detective Sergeant Richard Felber whether he was "satisfied that there was no sex motive behind the crime," Felber hesitated in his response, implying that investigators may not have completely eliminated that motive. However, prosecutor Murray quickly stood up and said that the "government is satisfied that there was no sex angle in the case." Thus, the prosecution took Fisher at his word that he had only removed her panties in a panic to clean up the blood. Still, it seems slightly odd, given that as a janitor he had plenty of cleaning supplies and he was obviously collected enough to break off his initial attack to fetch the firewood. As the janitor, why wouldn't he go fetch some actual cleaning supplies? Was there some sort of, perhaps subconscious, sexual humiliation at work, or did he genuinely just panic? A comment made by Fisher during the trial could reveal a great deal psychologically, or it could just be an offhand comment. When Houston asked him why he tore off Reardon's panties, Fisher replied, "I wanted to keep the place clean." Given that she had complained about him not keeping the place clean, degrading her in order to clean up her own blood from the building would certainly seem to be a way to get a satisfying, if disturbing, sense of revenge. Again, perhaps it was an almost subconscious act and he didn't fully realize why he did it. Throughout Fisher's calm and matter-of-fact recitation of events, an observer noted that several of the women on the jury "studiously avoided glancing at the defendant." During this portion of testimony, a visitor took a seat in the courtroom to listen: Robert Miller, a few weeks past his own time on the stand and evidently interested enough to pass his time between his own cases watching Fisher's.

Under questioning by Curran, Fisher elaborated on some of the statements in his confession. Curran brought up his claim that he suddenly decided to kill her because "her screaming done something to me. I had to stop that noise." Curran asked Fisher whether taking the time to go upstairs, decide what to do and select a weapon didn't suggest something beyond an impulsive act. Fisher replied, "No, her screams sort of pushed me towards the library fireplace. I picked up the wood and ran back downstairs." He said he was upstairs "about a minute." It does raise the question of what Reardon was doing while he was fetching the firewood, a point that rather oddly doesn't seem to have been addressed, at least in surviving testimony. Recall that Fisher said she ran to the back of her office area in the basement after he struck her initially, but it seems rather unlikely that her response to a smack from Fisher would be to then stand frozen in place, screaming, until he returned. Perhaps he gave her more than a "smack" and rendered her unable to flee. This would undercut his claim that her continued screams had a psychological hold on him that drove him upstairs to get a weapon. He certainly could have initially strangled her senseless, dropped her to the ground to create one of the fractures she sustained and then ran upstairs to get the firewood and deliver a second blow as she was on the ground. But it could also be argued that the facts just as easily suggested that he laid in wait with the piece of wood and ambushed her, although if he intended an ambush, the pistol he had in his possession at his arrest would be a much more likely weapon. Or it could have happened exactly as he told it. We can never know exactly what happened in those frantic last seconds of Reardon's life.

Curran wrapped up his questioning of Fisher regarding the murder, and the following rather crushing exchange occurred:

> *"You bludgeoned her?"*
> *"Yes."*
> *"You choked her?"*
> *"Yes."*
> *"You knifed her?"*
> *"Yes."*

"And yet you say you didn't really intend to kill her?"
"No."
"Well, you know you didn't do her any good."
"It doesn't seem so."

After depositing Reardon in the subbasement and trying to wipe up some of the blood, Fisher testified that he tried to calm down for a few moments and then went home on a streetcar. There, he tossed his own bloodstained clothes into his bedroom closet and went out for some beers after changing clothes, not giving his wife any hint of what had occurred. Returning home, he rolled up the bloody clothes and put them in the back of the closet to better hide them and at that time hid Reardon's ring as well. Fisher claimed that he didn't mean to take the ring at all, and it had just gotten stuck in his pocket as he dragged the body into the subbasement. It seems like a rather dubious explanation, and Fisher didn't explain why he saved the ring once he supposedly found it rather than dispose of it.

He described feeling "nervous as if I had a bad dream….I couldn't think of anything to do, so I stayed in bed until the next morning." Surviving court documents don't indicate whether he was asked about placing the mysterious call to police about a murdered woman in the Cathedral; perhaps they did clarify that odd event at trial. He spent the hours before his arrest on March 2 wandering around the city. He thought about turning himself in but couldn't muster up the courage to do so. His arrest followed that night.

Houston also tried to show that Fisher was not mentally responsible for his actions and could not have formed premeditation. In a faintly amusing misogynistic comment, one paper noted that a "psychiatrist and a woman psychologist" testified for the defense. The psychiatrist was Dr. Ernest Williams of Howard University, perhaps the most well-known Black psychiatrist in the country, and the "woman psychologist" was Dr. Astrea Campbell of the same institution. Campbell testified that an intelligence test showed Fisher had the mentality of someone who was eleven years and four months old, but her testimony was weakened when she admitted under cross-examination that the tests were scaled so that the highest attainable age was sixteen. Campbell also stated that Fisher had an IQ of seventy-six, which was "on the borderline of mental deficiency." According to Fisher, he hadn't finished the third grade and after leaving school held a variety of jobs, including chauffeur, elevator operator and exterminator, among others. (Reporters tracked down one company where he was employed as a truck driver and found that he was fired for "incompetency.") Williams "refused to state definitively" whether

Fisher was of sound mind at the time of the murder, but he didn't believe Fisher could tell between right and wrong "at the time of the crime [and] he couldn't resist an impulse to kill because of an unsound mind." Williams added his opinion that Fisher was a "psychopathic personality and suffered from acute alcoholism." According to Williams, people like that often have a "lack of aggressiveness…but when their emotions are aroused they have an overwhelming impulse to kill." Fisher was allowed to testify over government objections about his drinking habits and said he had been arrested several times for public drunkenness throughout two years of heavy drinking. Houston was using alcoholism as a subsidiary argument as to why Fisher wasn't in control of his actions on the day of the murder. While Fisher never claimed that he was drinking on the day of the murder, Fisher said that the night before the slaying, he went to several beer joints and "spent most of the night with a girl called Elaine." The prosecution called Dr. Edgar Griffin of St. Elizabeth's Hospital to offer a contrary opinion as to Fisher's mental state. He testified that though Fisher may have been provoked and angry, he knew the nature and quality of his actions when he killed Reardon.

Houston knew that he would not be able to prove that Fisher was legally insane, but he was trying to prove that Fisher had diminished responsibility for the crime and couldn't have formed premeditation based on his mental instability and limited intellect. The problem with this was that Justice Proctor limited the inclusion of much of this evidence regarding his mental state into jury consideration since the issue of insanity itself was not actually being debated. In most jurisdictions, juries could only consider whether the accused was legally sane and knew the difference between right and wrong, not whether the totality of their mental state may have disposed them toward committing a crime. Houston was asking Justice Proctor to bend that legal principle and let the jury consider whether a mental disturbance or limitation not meeting the insanity criteria entitled Fisher to a second-degree verdict.

After both sides closed their arguments, the case was briefly reopened for the defense to present new medical evidence from a doctor and a serologist that a spinal tap showed Fisher suffered from neuro-syphilis, affecting his mental state. Dr. Williams returned to the stand to say that someone with neuro-syphilis might have their brain tissues and sanity affected, but the government brought a medical technician from Gallinger Hospital to say that she saw no evidence of neuro-syphilis in the spinal fluid sample, and Dr. Griffin stated that Fisher definitely did not have cerebral syphilis. All in all, it was a fairly desperate last attempt to show Fisher to be mentally unbalanced.

In their closing arguments, Murray and Curran summarized their view that Fisher's repeated attempts to kill Reardon by various means, hide her body and clean up the scene showed that he was in control of his actions. While never arguing that Fisher shouldn't be punished, Houston argued that his client shouldn't be found guilty of first-degree murder because there was no motive, no robbery, no sex and he had "nothing to gain." He told the jury:

> *I am not arguing that Fisher should be turned loose on the street. We do not deny that Miss Reardon was brutally killed by him. But I do say that he was caught in a vise of fear. I say that if Miss Reardon had been colored or that Fisher had been white, there would have been no murder resulting from the argument and the first slap.... The whole thing can give you only a picture of a person who was not normal.*

Whether the jury would agree with his claims remained to be seen.

Following a conference with the attorneys, on June 29, Proctor instructed the jury that they could convict only on one of the two counts, murder by choking/strangling or murder by bludgeoning. Houston asked Proctor to let the jury consider certain aspects of the testimony regarding Fisher's mental abilities, as described, but Proctor declined. The jury wasn't gone long after starting their discussion at 4:40 p.m.; they took only forty minutes to reach a decision: guilty of first-degree murder. Fisher's face never changed from the "blank expression" it had throughout the trial. There were some awkward moments, as the jury had misunderstood Proctor's instructions and convicted him on both counts, so after conferring with the attorneys, Proctor sent them back to return with one verdict with the exasperated comment that "one cannot kill a human twice." After fifteen minutes, they returned to the "near-empty courtroom" and found him guilty of killing Catherine Reardon by choking and strangling her. Houston asked for the jurors to be polled, and several women's voices "trembled with emotion" as they gave their answer.

Houston announced that he would file for a new trial, claiming that Fisher was inadequately warned about the implications of his confession, there was unfavorable "spotlighting" of Fisher's testimony in jury instructions and, most importantly, some portions of the psychiatric testimony were not admitted into evidence. To no one's surprise, Proctor denied the motion. At his sentencing on July 7, Fisher said quietly, "Your honor, I'm very sorry this thing happened. I had no intent to do any killing." For the first time since being arrested, he showed emotion by closing his eyes and biting his lip as

Proctor sentenced him to die in the electric chair. Houston told the press that he would appeal the case, but the District Court of Appeals upheld the conviction. Justice Thurman Arnold upheld the lower court's refusal to include some portions of the testimony about Fisher's mental abilities and wrote that Fisher's decision to fetch the firewood to use as a weapon and then continue the attack to silence Reardon "showed a persistent purpose in the execution of the crime during an appreciable time."

Houston did not give up and appealed this decision to the U.S. Supreme Court, which agreed to hear the case. Thus, a modest janitor lent his name to *Fisher v. United States*. On April 23, 1945, in a 5–3 decision (one justice did not participate), the Supreme Court upheld the conviction. Justice Stanley Reed delivered the majority opinion, in which he said that Houston sought jury instructions that

> *would have permitted the jury to weigh the evidence of the defendant's mental deficiencies, which were a sort of insanity in the legal sense. The trial court refused and the United States Court of Appeals here upheld the refusal.…Matters relating to law enforcement in the District of Columbia and entrusted to the courts of the District. Our policy is not to interfere with the local rules of law which they fashion, save in exceptional situations where egregious error has been committed. Where the choice of the Court of Appeals of the District of Columbia in local matters between conflicting legal conclusions seems nicely balanced, we do not interfere.*

Justice Felix Frankfurter authored the dissenting opinion, in which he described Fisher as "a man of primitive emotions reacting to the sudden stimulus of insult and proceeding from that point without purpose or design." Frankfurter thought that the jury instructions didn't make the definition of premeditation clear enough or focus enough on the option of a second-degree conviction. Much more could be written on the legal aspects of *Fisher v. United States*, and a certain amount has been written over the years, but any further elaboration would be outside the scope of this book and the author's expertise.

Despite the failure at the Supreme Court, Houston gained Fisher another year and a half of life through a series of attempts to gain a rehearing with the Supreme Court and then for executive clemency. Nothing worked, although Fisher wasn't entirely without public support for a commutation. A newspaper editorial opined that given the relatively close 5–3 decision in the Supreme Court ruling, authorities should be cautious and commute his sentence to life imprisonment, for if "members of a court of last resort disagree," then it should indicate that no one could be very confident in the first-degree verdict. The editorial also referred to New York's policy of doing so in similar cases. However, there doesn't seem to have been a groundswell of support for such a commutation.

Not that it did him any good, but Fisher and another Black prisoner on death row named William Copeland were praised for not joining two white death row inmates in a dramatic 1946 escape from the District Jail. According to a reporter, the "colored men were convinced that the chance was not worth it in the long run, [they] thought that they would be breaking faith with the persons who were fighting for them and [they] believed they owed a duty to their wives, loyally standing by them." Fisher also told the reporter that an escape wouldn't help him much and "I could not think of anything but my wife and my friends who I know I would hurt too much."

A last attempt to gain executive clemency from Harry Truman was denied in December, and Fisher kept his appointment with the electric chair on December 20, 1946 (as did Copeland and another killer, Joseph Medley). Fisher's wife, Elizabeth, visited him in the District Jail the night before his execution. As the three men awaited their fate on the morning of the twentieth, a reporter noted that "[b]oth colored men and Medley appeared calm and resigned to their fate." William Copeland walked smilingly to the chair, smoking a cigar, and was electrocuted at 10:30 a.m. Fisher replaced him in the seat ten minutes later, and the reporter observed that "Fisher also walked to his death without assistance, keeping his eyes closed as he sat in the chair. He did not appear to say anything as the straps were adjusted." Another reporter thought that Fisher looked "pale, even through his dark skin," but agreed that he walked in calmly and briskly and then helped the guards strap him into the chair. The electricity was turned on at 10:45 a.m., and Julius Fisher was pronounced dead five minutes after that. His wife claimed his body. Julius Fisher would indirectly have something of an afterlife, as author Richard Wright was intrigued by the case and wrote a short story called "The Man Who Killed a Shadow" directly based on the murder. A copy of the Supreme Court decision exists with Wright's notes and annotations on it, and the story contains details identical to the actual murder, although Wright adds a rebuffed attempt at seduction by the story's murder victim as a way to engage in some societal commentary. Other than that, the story of the unusual murder in the Cathedral's shadow has largely drifted off into the haziness of time, unknown by the thousands of tourists who visit the Cathedral each year.

CHAPTER 5

EVIL STALKS ROCK CREEK PARK

No matter how many murder cases one reads about or researches, the murder of a child never ceases to be anything other than deeply and profoundly disturbing. Such an evil occurrence visited Rock Creek Park in 1948. Eleven-year-old Carol Bardwell, who had just finished the sixth grade at Sacred Heart School, was enjoying a pleasant school-free day on Sunday, June 27. Her father, William, was an investigator for the Federal Trade Commission, and her mother, Elizabeth, stayed home with Carol and an eight-month-old boy. Between 3:30 and 4:00 p.m., Carol asked her father for permission to go to a playground in nearby Rock Creek Park. From the Bardwell home at 1635 Webster Street, NW, where they had resided for twenty years, it was less than a mile to the playground, and she had been there many times before. Her father did tell her not to take a shortcut path through the woods to get there, though. She would ride her bike, a favorite present from last Christmas, to the park. William Bardwell expected her back in an hour or so in time for dinner; Carol was a responsible girl, and he had no reason to think she would stay out later than that. As she rode away, a fourteen-year-old friend saw her go by and shouted after her, but Carol evidently did not hear her and continued on her journey. The friend got her own bike and tried to catch up with Carol but couldn't find her and turned back, perhaps altering her or Carol's fate.

When over an hour passed without Carol's return, her father became worried. He searched the playground in Rock Creek Park near 16th Street without success, and when he returned home, his wife reminded him that there was another playground just south of that, closer to 17th Street. He checked the second playground and then walked back to his house using the shortcut trail he had told Carol not to take. The trail ran northwest–southeast and connected a baseball field to Colorado Avenue near 17th Street. About one hundred yards from Colorado, he must have felt a rising sense of panic; at the side of the trail was Carol's bike. Based on the fact that it was facing toward Colorado, she had presumably abandoned the bike on her way home. Why she had abandoned it was the disturbing question William Bardwell had to confront. After looking around for a few minutes, he decided the police needed to be contacted immediately. He went to a friend's house nearby, taking Carol's bike with him, and called the police. Word quickly circulated throughout the neighborhood, and residents immediately proceeded to Rock Creek Park to search for Carol. The Bardwells were a popular family, and their friends did not hesitate to search for the likable girl. A neighbor later said that Carol was "a girl everybody loved," and another neighbor said that she was a careful girl, so everyone was immediately concerned at her absence. A Park Police officer took the Bardwells into his car and drove around the park, searching for the girl, while other police cars and motorcycles searched as well.

As the search began, John Breen was enjoying a stroll through Rock Creek Park with Lucille Bengstrom, unaware of the unfolding drama. About 7:50 p.m., the pair was walking on the same shortcut trail that William Bardwell had recently traversed. Something off the trail caught Breen's attention.

Carol's house still stands; she departed here on her bike and cycled down the street to the left. *Author's collection.*

In what would prove to be very near the spot one hundred yards northwest of Colorado Avenue where Bardwell had found Carol's bike, Breen stepped off the trail to investigate and was horrified to see the body of a young girl about thirty feet off the trail. The body was doubled up on its side and partially hidden by a fallen tree. Breen and Bengstrom quickened their pace toward Colorado Avenue and almost immediately encountered Daniel Johnson, one of the neighbors searching for Carol. It was clear that Johnson was searching for someone, so Breen assumed that Johnson must be the father of the young girl he had just found, and he excitedly told him not to go any farther. Johnson explained who he was, and after telling the grandsons who accompanied him to stay back, he followed Breen to the body. Johnson undoubtedly knew that he was about to see the body of Carol Bardwell, but it did not lessen the shock of the horrifying scene that he observed. Johnson later said that the body "was covered with blood but I recognized her at once. I couldn't stand to get within 15 feet of her....She was lying in a pool of half-dried blood....Her dress was just above her knees but she was not exposed." Johnson quickly went to a friend's house and called the police to update them on the situation.

Officers from both the Park Police and the Metropolitan Police immediately descended on the scene; the Metropolitan Police and its detective force would lead the investigation. Police chief Robert Barrett was called at his beach cottage and immediately returned to D.C. Detectives approached the body and saw that there were broken tree limbs and brush near the body, leading them to conclude that the murder occurred within a few feet of where she was found. There were no signs of a significant struggle, though, so police thought the killer must have quickly snatched Carol, covered her mouth and dragged her into the woods before killing her. A shocked William Bardwell was brought to the scene to identify the body, while police and friends intercepted Elizabeth Bardwell en route and prevented her from seeing her daughter. Two priests accompanied her home to comfort her. Coroner A. Magruder MacDonald (a man we have already met more than once) was immediately called to the scene to examine the body; he arrived by 8:30 p.m. The girl he examined was five feet, three inches tall and weighed about 110 pounds. She wore a white dress with black stripes; on the slip underneath it were pinned four religious medals, evidence of the devoutly Catholic family she belonged to. She wore white sneakers, and on a string around her neck was a key to the family's garage; she wore a silver identification bracelet on her left wrist. MacDonald found that there were two slight abrasions on the bridge of her nose and left chest, probably from contact with the

Left: Carol's father saw this view when he found her bike. The trail she rode on is now a paved access road; her body was found to the right of the road. *Author's collection.*

Below: There is still a playground in the same location as in 1948. Carol spent the last few moments of her life here and then headed toward the trees in the background. *Author's collection.*

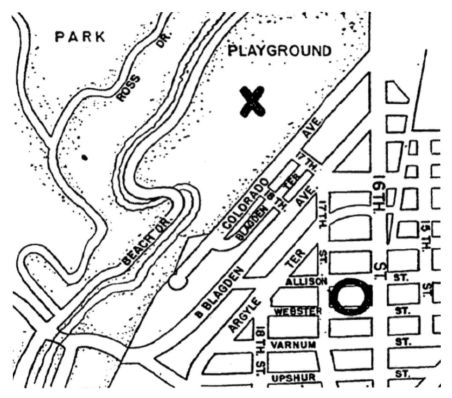

Carol Bardwell's house is circled on the right of the map, the playground she visited is labeled near the top and the crime scene is marked by an X. *Courtesy of* Washington Evening Star.

ground during a struggle. Two scratches on her chest that MacDonald called "minute" may have been caused by fingernails.

It was not difficult to determine the cause of death; her throat had been slashed almost ear to ear with what seemed like one stroke. The jugular vein was severed, leading to extensive pools of blood found on either side of the body; her blonde hair was matted with blood. Her windpipe had not been cut. MacDonald thought that the knife that cut her throat had a narrow blade, and his initial impression was that she had been dead for about two hours. However, after conducting the autopsy, he more definitively placed her death at about four hours before he examined the body. In other words, Carol was killed around 4:30 or 5:00 p.m., a time that coincided with what William Bardwell said about her trip to the playground. Based on his initial examination at the scene, MacDonald told police that Carol hadn't been sexually assaulted. The condition of her clothes was ambiguous, as

The spot where Carol's body was found remains a quiet, isolated glade in the woods, hiding its terrible history. *Author's collection.*

they were not torn and her dress's position above her knees could have just occurred if the body was dragged or moved around. However, when he had the chance to examine the body at the morgue, he changed his mind and immediately requested what he called "a chemical test." It is not difficult to guess what exactly MacDonald was looking for on Carol's body. Based on the results of that test and his own more thorough examination, on June 30, MacDonald told the press that Carol had in fact been sexually assaulted, though he couldn't determine if it happened before or after death. Following the autopsy, Carol's clothes were dispatched to the FBI for further analysis. Carol's funeral service was held on July 1 at the Shrine of the Sacred Heart following a prayer service at the Bardwell home. Many classmates and teachers were present, and one teacher paid tribute to the well-behaved girl, saying that her teachers often said that they "wished the other children were like Carol." Carol's schoolmates lined the entrance to the nearly full church as the body was taken to Mount Olivet Cemetery for burial. As a final tribute, the Bardwells gave Children's Hospital a painting and plaque in Carol's memory called "Oh, Come Let Us Sing Unto the Lord." The Bardwells could offer little help to detectives; William Bardwell told them Carol was a shy girl, and he didn't think she would have willingly stopped to talk to a stranger. He also sadly noted that Carol was originally supposed to go to a movie with a friend, but when the friend had to cancel the movie trip, she had gone on her fatal trip to the playground instead.

The crime scene yielded little evidence. The path where the crime occurred was an old, unpaved road that local children often used as a shortcut to the developed trail system within Rock Creek Park. About five hundred feet northwest of the crime scene, the path connected with a bridle trail that ran through the park. It was a bold crime; scores of people were within a few hundred yards of the murder site, picnicking or using the nearby recreational facilities just north and east of the scene. Police figured that other people must have unknowingly passed by the murder site before Breen noticed the body. Fifty police officers combed Rock Creek Park for clues, and they found a man's hat and several empty whiskey bottles but determined that they didn't have any connection to the crime. The searchers borrowed a mine detector from the army to search for the murder weapon, but with no luck. Carol's bicycle was checked for fingerprints, but none proved to be unidentified, belonging to Carol, her mother and several friends who police tracked down and cleared. Police officers checked laundries throughout D.C. for any bloody clothes that had been turned in for cleaning, but every owner of bloody clothes proved to have a solid alibi. Police learned that a handyman employed in the neighborhood had left the house where he was working at about the time that Carol headed to the park. The next morning, he didn't show up for work. It was enough for the police to take him into custody and question him. Forty-one-year-old Douglas Guiles, a Black man, told investigators his activities on the day in question. Police weren't completely satisfied with his alibi but determined that he had nothing to do with Carol's murder; they were thorough enough that they compared lipstick stains found on his shirt to the kind that Carol sometimes wore. They didn't match, and one suspects the lipstick stains had something to do with his suspicious alibi. The *Washington Afro American* editorialized that the *Washington Times Herald* in particular focused on the race of the handyman and other suspects and accused that paper of trying to fan racial flames that could lead to a race riot.

All other avenues were pursued to frustrating ends. Investigators visited nearby Walter Reed Hospital to see if it had any psychiatric patients who might have been out of the hospital that Sunday. There were no leads there, but detectives spoke to an escaped patient from the mental ward at Fort Belvoir Hospital who was found wandering around D.C. and muttering, "Poor little girl, why did he murder her?" Detectives concluded he had nothing to do with the case. All knife-related incidents logged by the police in the seventy-two hours before the murder were rechecked for any connection. Detectives made the usual check of local sex offenders and spoke with a teenager who had been arrested in September for trying to molest a young woman on a bike near where Carol was killed. By July 2, over one hundred people had been questioned in the case, but nothing brought any clarity. Undercover female police officers were stationed throughout Rock Creek Park in a desperate effort to lure perverts into the open, without result.

A seemingly strong tip came in when a witness reported that she had seen three Black girls running out of the park at about 6:40 p.m. on the night of Carol's murder just past where the body was found. One of the girls shouted, "Why did we come here, anyway?" Another of the girls said that they should catch a bus. After hearing of Carol's murder, the witness concluded that they may have seen the body or killer and fled in a panic. The three girls were finally tracked down and questioned on July 5. They could not offer any information on the murder; they had simply been playfully racing for the bus when the witness saw them. Police took them to Rock Creek Park to see if their memories could be jogged to recall something of relevance to the case, but nothing useful emerged. In an interesting insight on racial tensions of the time, newspaper coverage makes clear that the girls were sought as witnesses, not suspects, but more than one article in the *Washington Afro American* portrays the police as seeking the girls as suspects in the murder. The reality of racial persecution in other cases led to an incorrect perception; there is absolutely nothing in police statements or media coverage to suggest anyone thought of the girls as possible subjects. Another witness saw a man with a bloody shirt and face between 4:30 and 5:00 p.m. at 14th Street and Park Road NW, trying to hitch a ride. He was described as thirty-five years old, five feet nine or ten inches, 155 pounds, thin, with sharp or oval features and light brown hair. With little else to go on, police would be on the lookout for anyone in the park matching this general description. A second report that a bloody person was seen in the park on the day of the murder also came in, this time sending police looking for a fourteen- to fifteen-year-old boy with bloody clothes.

The press recognized that investigators were doing all they could to track down the murderer, but an editorial in the *Washington Evening Star* complained of inadequate police numbers in Rock Creek Park, tallying the Park Police force as having ninety-two officers to cover six thousand acres throughout D.C. A *Washington Post* editorial brought up a different complaint, saying that having separate Park Police and Metropolitan Police forces was harming the investigation. However, the two forces seemed to cooperate well, and another article pointed out that there were many different specialized police forces throughout the capital. Eventually, a bill was introduced in Congress to merge the Park Police into the Metropolitan Police, but it was not passed. During the introduction of the bill, one congressman, perhaps subconsciously thinking of his own organization, declared that D.C. was "the haven of sexual perverts and criminals." For its part, the Park Police asked for funding for more mounted police, and Congress recommended that forty officers be added to the force. Taking matters into their own hands, a number of residents near the murder site acquired dogs for protection, leading to a serious enough rise in barking complaints that a newspaper article was written on the matter.

Park Police continued to monitor the park in hopes that the killer might return to the scene. One darkly comic moment emerged when a man was arrested while lurking near the crime scene. After five hours of questioning, he proved to just be an amateur sleuth who was trying to solve the case himself. The would-be detective enjoyed the interrogation so much that he refused to leave police headquarters once he was released from custody! Multiple reports of strange and frightening behavior in Rock Creek Park reached police, but ultimately, they proved nothing other than that a disconcerting number of weird and perverted men roamed the area. A woman reported that a half-nude man tried to molest her in the park on June 29, which brought police to determine if there was a connection to the crime. Other reports of a semi-nude man in the park the next evening brought police rushing in, but to no avail. On the evening of July 3, a woman and her husband were out looking for a lost dog on Spring Road, about fifteen blocks from the murder site, when a man jumped out of some bushes and grabbed the woman. She screamed, and the man fled into Rock Creek Park, pursued by the victim's husband. She described the attacker as five foot nine, slender and slightly balding, which broadly matched the report of the bloody man police were seeking. The man was never tracked down, nor was a man who reportedly was cruising around in a car with Maryland plates, following young girls in the park. Detective Chief Robert Bryant personally went along on patrols through the park, desperate to find any clue that would lead to Bardwell's killer, but leads quickly dried up. Local citizen groups raised a $900 reward to draw out tips, but it proved no more successful than the police patrols in tracking down Carol's killer. The *Washington Times Herald* dramatically upped the ante by offering a $5,000 reward for the capture of the child murderer. Despite this, no significant tips came in, and police admitted to the press that they were no closer to solving the case than when they began. On July 7, Carol's mother, Betty, wrote an anguished message to the public, published in the *Washington Times Herald*. She wrote how as parents they tried to balance freedom and safety for Carol, and how it took only one decision by Carol to take the shortcut through the woods to lead to a fateful encounter with her killer. Betty begged parents to watch their children closely: "Keep a close watch over them—now more than ever—and you will then feel you've done all you can."

Around 10:00 p.m. on July 7, an officer spotted a man in Rock Creek Park near 16th Street who matched the description of a suspicious person spotted in the park earlier that day. In that less-regulated era of policing, when the man refused the officer's demand that he stop, the officer fired two shots at the fleeing man. Two hours later, another officer on patrol in the park spotted the man again as he ran out from under a bridge. When he again refused to stop, this officer had the same response as the first and fired a couple of shots in the man's direction. The man was never tracked down, but presumably the trigger-happy officers had discouraged his nocturnal visits to the park.

Unexpectedly, the case broke wide open, but it would happen in the worst way possible. On the day of the shooting misadventures in the park on July 7, D.C. police received news of a crime that had occurred in Baltimore the day before. It immediately piqued their interest. About forty miles away in Baltimore, July 6 offered an enjoyable summer vacation day for local children. Eleven-year-old Marsha Brill, a sixth grader at Arlington School, was riding her bike with friend Barbara Lee Sapperstein, also eleven, and Barbara's eight-year-old brother Alan. The trio rode down Glen Avenue between Cross Country Boulevard and Park Heights Avenue. Although not far from their homes, this stretch of Glen Avenue was not yet developed and was lined with woods. From where the children were biking, the closest homes were about one hundred yards away on Merville Avenue. It was a great stretch of road for biking, with little traffic and a hill for coasting down. Around 12:30 p.m., Marsha and Barbara were at the bottom of the hill when Alan started riding back up it. Suddenly, a Black man stepped out of the woods and seemed to collide with Marsha. Her bike fell to the ground, and she began to run away in a zigzag fashion, screaming and clutching her stomach, with the man in pursuit. Barbara began pedaling up the hill as fast as she could, away from the man. While not fully comprehending what was happening, Barbara and Alan were understandably terrified. Dr. Marvin Graham, a local dentist, happened to be driving down Glen Avenue when he saw two children on bikes pedaling in his direction. They stopped and began waving frantically and shouting something. Puzzled but assuming the children were just fooling around, Dr. Graham drove a few yards farther on when he saw a bicycle lying in the road near the intersection with Merville Avenue. Realizing that something was not right, he stopped and then heard what sounded like crying. He saw a young girl sitting by the side of the road at the edge of the tree line, hunched over and covered in blood. He immediately ran to her and asked what was wrong. Crying with pain, she managed to reply, "A colored man hit me." Making a logical assumption, Graham asked, "With a car?" but received a disturbing reply: "No, with a knife." Knowing that a local doctor's office was nearby, Graham scooped up Marsha and put her in his front seat. Dr. Jonas Cohen was not in his office on Park Avenue, but his nurse was there and administered first aid to Marsha while Graham called an ambulance. On the ride to the doctor's office, Marsha was lucid enough to give Graham her phone number, and the dentist called her mother as well. Still bewildered by the situation he had stumbled into and not wanting to panic Mrs. Brill, he told her that Marsha "had an accident" and that she needed to go to Union Memorial Hospital. By now the nurse had made clear that Marsha was suffering from a serious stab wound, and Graham called the police. The Good Samaritan had made a valiant effort, but it was to no avail; Marsha died either on the ambulance ride to the hospital or just after arriving there.

After failing to wave down Dr. Graham, Barbara and Alan Sapperstein shortly succeeded in getting the next passing car to stop, shouting to the startled occupants that "a colored man is stabbing Marsha." The driver was not a local and didn't know the area, but she waved down a passing man in a truck who took the children and their bikes to their nearby home, and another call was placed to the police. In response to the two calls about a child being stabbed, every available police car in Baltimore descended on the scene and began searching for the suspect. The Sapperstein children gave a basic description of the Black man and said he was wearing a blue shirt and dungarees. Soon, 250 police officers were searching the northwest part of the city in what was described as the greatest manhunt in Baltimore's history. Within two hours, police had arrested a Black man emerging from some woods about ten blocks from the murder scene. Although held and questioned for two days, the man was released when he provided an alibi from his employer. The scene itself didn't yield many clues. A trail of blood led from Marsha's bike eighty-five yards to near the intersection of Glen Avenue and Merville Avenue where Graham had found her, tracking her terrified flight from her killer. A pool of blood was next to the bike, and in the midst of it was a full impression of Marsha's hand but nothing that would point to who her killer was. Marsha's autopsy showed that she had a slash or "gaping stab wound" 1.0 inch wide, 2.25 inches long and 1.25 inches deep to the right side of her chest. The wound cut through one rib and partly cut through another before it punctured a lobe of the liver. Hemorrhages in her stomach and breast were the direct cause of death.

The same wave of tragedy that flowed through Carol Bardwell's neighborhood now went through Marsha Brill's. A school friend spoke fondly of Marsha, saying that "[a]ll the boys liked her because…she was so pretty and because she was so nice to everybody. She was even nice to her little sister." Several people commented about how musically inclined she was. Neighbors noted that her father, a grocery store owner, had moved his family to their current house a year earlier after living in an apartment above the store. Neighbors and local businesses quickly raised a $1,500 reward for the apprehension of her killer. The Brills were Jewish, and Marsha went to Beth Jacob Hebrew School three times a week in addition to her other schooling. Her Girl Scout troop planned to furnish a recreation room at the school in her memory. Her grandmother spoke to a reporter and sadly noted that Marsha was preparing to attend a summer camp where she worked. Marsha had visited the camp several days prior and liked it so much that she wanted to stay. Her grandmother reproached herself, saying, "I should have let her stay. I did have sixteen grandchildren. Now I have fifteen. I should have let her stay." Three hundred people attended Marsha's Orthodox Jewish funeral; burial followed at Sadova Congregation Cemetery at Herring Run, where her parents had to be physically supported to keep from collapsing.

The identity of Marsha Brill's murderer did not stay hidden long due to a critical tip. The story of the murder was splashed across the pages of Baltimore's evening paper the day it occurred, and Milton Elmore, a policeman temporarily assigned as a mechanic in the police garage, read about the disturbing case. The description of a Black man wielding a knife jogged his memory about a man he had arrested in 1940. This man was convicted of nonfatal assaults with a knife on two women in northwest Baltimore amid a spree of fifteen reported knife attacks. Elmore wasn't sure if he was still in prison, but he decided that detectives needed to check into this man. That man was Eugene "Bunky" James, a thirty-one-year-old Black janitor and handyman. Investigators immediately pulled up James's file; sure enough, he had recently been paroled. While it was a solid tip, detectives had many similar tips about men convicted in other crimes, and James was simply added to the list of men to talk to. At about 11:00 p.m., they fetched him from his home at 3311 Paton Avenue, which police noted was about one and a half miles from the site of the Brill murder, and held him in custody overnight until they could question him on July 7.

Meanwhile, D.C. and Baltimore police began communicating with each other. Detectives working the Bardwell case were understandably interested in hearing about a second eleven-year-old girl stabbed to death while riding a bike. As of yet, there was nothing physical to link the two crimes. Near Marsha's body, detectives found a souvenir badge from the Wilson Line's SS *Mount Vernon*, an excursion boat that plied the Potomac from D.C. to an amusement park and recreational area at Marshall Hall, Maryland. While the badge suggested a possible connection to D.C., detectives did not think it was connected to the case, and they eventually were proved correct. Still, Washington police remained keenly interested in the Brill case and prepared to visit their Baltimore colleagues.

Police questioning of James began. Standing five feet, seven inches tall and weighing about 140 pounds, he didn't look very intimidating. However, his police record showed that he had been arrested in Baltimore on June 2,

1940, for assault, robbery and burglary. While out on bond, he was again arrested just a week later for robbery, assault to rob and assault to murder. Fifteen white women in the same general area of northwest Baltimore had been assaulted with knives and sometimes robbed, and it didn't take long for a court to find that Eugene James was the guilty man in at least some of the cases. Convicted for two of the attacks, James was sentenced to two concurrent ten-year terms. He started his sentence in the state penitentiary and then, in December 1943, was moved to the Roxbury Penal Farm before being paroled on December 23, 1947, after gaining time off for good behavior and work credits. The parole was part of a traditional "Christmas commutation" of soon-to-be released prisoners.

Following Marsha's murder, detectives questioned James, but in spite of his suspicious past, they didn't gain any information that particularly set him apart from other men they were questioning. He was about to be released when Captain Clarence Forrester walked into the room where James was being questioned. Something caught his attention: James was wearing a crucifix and black rosary beads around his neck. The crucifix rang a bell for Forrester; thinking for a moment, he remembered that on June 15, a thirty-eight-year-old woman had reported being waylaid by a Black man, taken into some woods and then raped and robbed. Something that stuck in her mind was the crucifix that her rapist was wearing, and Forrester thought that her description of it sounded an awful lot like the one that James was wearing just then. It was enough for Forrester to ask more questions of James. Police decided to hold him overnight and continue his questioning on July 8. Investigators started with the June 15 rape and robbery. James initially told them, "You've got nothing on me," but it wasn't long before he confessed to the attack. He likewise denied killing Brill, but after going through his claimed whereabouts on July 6, police caught him in some improbable statements, and James quickly broke down. He admitted that he saw the children on bikes and said that "this dizzy spell came down on me and I don't remember nothing," but he then proceeded to offer details about the murder.

James led police to the location where he buried the knife he said he used. He first led them on a meandering journey in search of a chisel and sharp stick he claimed he was carrying at the time of Marsha's murder. After realizing he was taking them on a wild goose chase, officers searched his home, and though they didn't find a knife, bloodstained dungaree trousers and a shirt were found in the basement of the home, matching what the Sappersteins reported seeing. It looked like someone had tried to wash the pants. James then suddenly decided to tell the truth and take them to the murder weapon. It was a pattern he would repeat from the moment he was first questioned: tell rather transparent lies and then quickly tell the truth when questioned more closely about the lies. The burial site proved to be near Whitney Avenue and Key Avenue, about a three-and-a-half-block walk from Marsha Brill's murder location. James led police into the woods, and twenty-five or thirty feet into the trees, he showed them a rock located between two sticks pushed vertically into the ground. The knife was buried a foot underneath the crude marker. It proved to be a dirty, rusty butcher knife with a six-inch "very narrow blade," just as Coroner MacDonald had predicted in Carol Bardwell's murder. James said he thought it was "supposed to be an old Japanese knife, but it looks like a butcher knife to me," and said that he had found it three weeks earlier while burning trash at the apartment building where he was employed.

The top police officials in Baltimore accompanied him to the crime scene, and he walked them through his version of the killing. The press quickly got wind of the crime scene visit, and a crowd of several hundred people began to congregate before James returned to police headquarters to give a full written statement. His confession was a mix of convincing details and unlikely statements; police typed his confession in a question-and-answer format and then had him sign it at about 10:00 p.m. on July 8. At three points during the confession, officers asked him if his statement was being made voluntarily and of his own free will, to which James agreed that it was. During his confession, James used a pencil to show how he stabbed Brill. Baltimore authorities immediately began to prepare for grand jury proceedings, with an indictment already forthcoming on July 9.

Oddly, Baltimore residents found out very little about James's confession before his trial due to a local contempt of court law passed in 1939 that barred the media from reporting statements made by accused persons before their trial. The intent was to give the accused the most fair-minded jurors possible, but there were clearly First Amendment issues at play. Several radio stations decided to use the Brill murder as a test case and reported on James's confession, although the local papers were not as bold. The result was that five radio stations were charged with "embarrassing and obstructing the administration of justice," prompting nationwide criticism from the American Civil Liberties Union and multiple other groups. The stations were convicted, but upon appeal, the convictions were overturned as the court deemed the gag rule to be unconstitutional. Not giving up, the Maryland attorney general went to the Supreme Court, which declined to review the appellate court's decision. Thus, Eugene James was the unwitting catalyst for increased freedom of speech in Baltimore.

By now, three detectives from D.C. had arrived, and after Baltimore police were satisfied with James's confession to Brill's murder, they gave the D.C. officers a chance to interrogate him. Besides the obvious similarity in the Brill and Bardwell killings, a remark by James during his interrogation by Baltimore police caught the attention of D.C. detectives. As James described his travels on the day of Brill's murder, a detective commented that he must walk a lot. James responded, "Yes, I even walked over to Washington." The D.C. detectives' questioning followed a similar pattern as the previous interrogation; after several hours of back-and-forth discussion leading nowhere, D.C. detective Robert Murray asked James to account for his actions on June 27 in detail. James named a couple in Baltimore he claimed he spent the day with. Murray then asked him to describe the day before and after Bardwell's murder; James stumbled over his answers and couldn't offer a coherent accounting of those days. After pointing out how suspicious it was that James could remember what he was doing on the day of the murder but not any other, Murray told James that detectives would check out his supposed alibi. With that, James abruptly gave up and confessed to killing Carol and admitted that the buried knife was also used to kill her. He freely admitted that he would likely kill more children if he wasn't kept in custody. His confession was typed up and then signed by him. He certainly had a strange tale to relate about that June day.

According to James, he went to a 6:00 a.m. mass at St. Ambrose Church in Baltimore, although priests were quick to distance themselves from James by telling police that he was not on their parish roll and no one remembered seeing him on June 27. He then returned home for a cup of coffee and, much more ominously, fetched his knife. He told police that "I just had an impulse to take a little trip," certainly an odd thing to do on the spur of the moment since he claimed that he hadn't been to D.C. since 1940. (He also stated that he spent a month in D.C. in 1939.) He hopped a freight train at 7:30 a.m., slipping into a gondola car, and headed to D.C., getting off at the Pennsylvania Railroad freight yards. He then described a day walking around D.C., visiting the Navy Yard, Justice Building and White House before deciding that he "wanted to see the gorillas" at the National Zoo. He asked several people near the White House if there were any gorillas at the zoo, and no one knew, so he asked directions to the zoo to see for himself. (Reporters later noted that there were not, in fact, any gorillas at the zoo.) Getting over whatever disappointment he felt at not seeing the gorillas, after visiting other animals at the zoo, he said that he spent two hours watching swans in a pond, completely transfixed. Shaking himself out of his swan-induced reverie, he headed into Rock Creek Park. Ominously, he had his knife tucked into his waistband and covered up by his shirt; he pretended it was a saber as he traipsed through the wooded park. At what he thought was about 5:00 p.m., as he walked along a footpath his attention went to a young girl standing next to a bicycle. In his mind, the girl "loomed up" in front of him. Some sort of impulse came over him, and he had an urge to attack the girl. He claimed he was walking in the opposite direction that Carol was riding in, and he tried to give the impression that he was just going to walk past her. (However, given his route from the zoo through the park, a more likely route would seemingly be southbound, in the same direction as Carol on her trip home, suggesting that he may have in fact been following her.) As he came up to her, he lunged at her and slashed her throat twice, once on each side of the neck.

The details he gave in his four-page statement convinced detectives that he was telling the truth; they had intentionally withheld any description of Carol's bike from the press. James described it accurately: blue and white with a woven wood basket. He also gave accurate details of Carol's appearance that had never been reported by the press, particularly the way her hair was braided and pinned. He always denied raping Carol but admitted experiencing "sexual gratification" when he slashed her throat. (He likewise always claimed that rape was not on his mind when it came to Marsha Brill.) Afterward, he said that a white couple walking down the trail came so close to him while he lurked in the trees where Carol's body was found that he could have reached out and touched them. He said that he wiped the knife clean with a handkerchief and then threw the handkerchief away, but police never found it. Once the coast was clear, he found that he was hot and sweaty, so he walked to a nearby stream, presumably Rock Creek, and washed his face. He then left the park, concerned that people walking behind him suspected something. He insisted that there wasn't blood on his clothes and that he wasn't the bloody man seen by witnesses. As he walked back to the freight yards to hop on another train, he claimed that he realized what he'd done and "felt bad." He arrived back in Baltimore about 8:00 p.m., went home to his mother and two sisters and then walked about a mile to bury the knife. The next day, he retrieved the knife and hid it under his mattress, and he then used it to kill Brill before reburying it following her murder. Parts of his story didn't quite ring true to the detectives, but the specific details he gave on some points convinced them that they had their man.

James soon offered more concrete evidence to support his confession. When D.C. detectives expressed doubt as to his knowledge of Rock Creek Park, James replied, "Give me a paper and pencil," and proceeded to draw them what police called a "crude but fairly accurate" diagram of the park in relation to Carol Bardwell's murder site. James proudly signed the diagram when he was finished. It showed the zoo and a road leading to Rock Creek Park and then accurately placed the location of her bike and body. He also sketched the path where he said he hid from the passing couple. Police also began investigating the bloodstained clothes found at James's home. Testing of the blood found that some of it did not match his blood type or Marsha Brill's, but sure enough, it matched Carol Bardwell's blood type.

Although at least one Black man who wrote into the *Washington Times Herald* felt as though all people of his race were being blamed for James's action, much like the *Afro American* editorial writer mentioned earlier, media coverage of the case didn't particularly play up a racial angle to the murders. While a grainy snapshot of James was included in newspaper coverage and he was frequently referred to as "colored" or as a "Negro," that was typical for a Black person referred to in any sort of newspaper article from that era, criminal or not. Another article in the Black paper described how bus riders were subjected to "Gestapo-like tactics" by police one day, and the riders assumed they were working on the Bardwell case, although a detective told the paper his officers were searching for a jail escapee. No doubt there was public opinion rooted in prejudice in a case of a Black man murdering two white girls, but the media generally stayed above this. One example of prejudice did surface in the context of a D.C. Recreation Department public meeting where it was proposed that Park View Playground be used during school hours by white children and by Black children at other times. The head of a neighborhood association argued that the Bardwell case was a reason the playground should not be turned over to Black people, implying that there would be an increase in crime. Alice Hunter, a Recreation Department employee in the meeting, responded, "As a Negro woman I resent that every time someone has been murdered the immediate thought is that a Negro committed it." While a good response, it undoubtedly would have changed more minds in the meeting had the reports of a Black man killing Carol not proved to be true. Another potential media controversy was narrowly avoided. When word reached the press of James's "Christmas commutation," rumblings of controversy began, with people assuming that had James not been paroled, he would still have been in prison, unable to kill. The indignation manifested itself in multiple letters to newspapers complaining about James's release. Governor William Lane of Maryland received pointed enough criticism in the *Washington Times Herald* that he wrote a letter in response, explaining that James was due to be released on January 3, 1948, and it was a custom to commute the last few days of a prisoner's sentence if they were scheduled to be released within the two weeks after Christmas. He added that James had been eligible for parole in October 1943 but had been denied.

While there was never any question that Baltimore would prosecute James for the Brill murder first, D.C. authorities wanted to convene a grand jury and at least have an indictment on file for James. Convened on July 15, the grand jury attempted to parse out the parts of James's confession that didn't seem quite right. By now, James claimed that while he remembered signing something in the presence of police, he didn't know what it said. A reporter for the *Washington Times Herald* managed to interview James in his cell, and the accused man claimed that detectives "put words in my mouth I didn't say.…I didn't know what was in the papers I signed." He claimed that the last time he was in D.C. was in 1939, when he worked for the Works Progress Administration on U Street. He added that while D.C. detectives didn't force him to sign the confession, Baltimore officers "kicked me several times." Regarding the evidence that he accurately described Carol's bike, he claimed that detectives showed him a picture of the bike and described it and then added the information to his confession. When the reporter asked about the "sexual gratification" he said he achieved when killing Carol, his somewhat odd response was, "I'm not queer. I am a normal person who has the same sexual desires as anyone else." The interview ended after the reporter could get no more information from James, as every question about the Bardwell murder was answered with some variation of "I wasn't there."

James declined to testify at the grand jury hearing. Inspector Joseph Itzel of the Baltimore police was brought to the grand jury hearing to corroborate the D.C. detectives' statements that the confession was freely given by James. James continually denied raping Carol; recall that Coroner MacDonald's initial impression was that no sexual assault had occurred, but upon a more detailed examination and lab tests, he decided that one had. At the grand jury, MacDonald insisted that he had "conclusive proof" as to the rape and it was now "apparent the child had been molested." Another comment he made seems to resolve the puzzle. MacDonald said that it was essential to know James's definition of rape. It can be clearly inferred that James had not completed the act of full intercourse but had assaulted Carol in some way and left evidence of it. James's admission of "sexual gratification" would also seem to be in line with this. Perhaps also important is the later discovery by psychiatrists that James had a "physical sexual deformity," which, besides its psychological implications, perhaps had something to do with the ambiguous nature of the assault. While MacDonald believed that Carol's throat was slashed once, he conceded that James's version of events could be true. If he had slashed her throat from each side and they met in the middle, it would look like one cut.

The grand jury also had to consider issues with James's account of his train ride to D.C. Investigators checked freight train schedules for the Baltimore and Ohio and Pennsylvania Railroads and didn't find a 7:30 a.m. train departing the Baltimore freight yard. Police had to consider whether his story was inaccurate or whether he simply misjudged the time; detectives noted that he didn't own a watch. Investigators initially found that the earliest train he could have caught in the Baltimore freight yard would have brought him to the D.C. rail yard at 1:30 p.m. However, upon further investigation, detectives found that there was indeed a train James could have caught at the time he claimed. Pennsylvania Railroad officials found that a train left at 7:23 a.m. from the Bay View freight yard on Maryland Avenue in Baltimore, where James could have climbed down a small embankment to board the train. Officials initially didn't give information about this train to investigators since it was normally scheduled to leave Baltimore at 2:00 a.m., but further investigation on delayed trains showed that it had been delayed for over five hours that day. This train arrived at the Anacostia freight yards, where James claimed to have gotten off, at 8:55 a.m. While this was a significant discovery by police, a witness muddled this issue at the grand jury hearing. Hilda Wiser was a train crossing guard in Lanham, Maryland, responsible for ensuring that the track crossing was safe. Wiser contacted police because after seeing a picture of James in the paper, she was convinced she had seen him on June 27, the day of the Bardwell murder, riding in a low-slung coal car as a freight train slowly rode by her crossing station. This matched James's account of the day, for he said that he rode in a coal gondola, but Wiser put the sighting at 10:00 a.m., which didn't match either the morning or the afternoon train he could have caught. She insisted that she "could pick him out of a thousand men." Although she could only see the top of his shoulders and head, she was sure that it was James. She explained that as part of her job, she was "supposed to look for hot boxes and bad axles and things like that, and we notice everything that goes on," hence why she noticed a man riding in the coal car. Wiser also claimed that she saw James on his return journey, but she said it occurred at about 10:30 a.m. on the twenty-eighth, not the evening of twenty-seventh, as James claimed. To support her credibility, Wiser told the grand jury that she had worked at the crossing for twenty-six years and noted that two years earlier she had spotted a man riding a freight train that she thought resembled a wanted burglary suspect. When she called police, they brushed off her sighting, only to find that when he was later arrested, he confirmed that he had been the man seen by Wiser. She also proudly related how in 1945, three men in pajamas and bathrobes came to her watchbox asking for directions, and suitably suspicious, she called police to arrest the men, who proved to be escapees from a prison hospital. The grand jury would have to decide what to make of Wiser's story or indeed consider how much it really mattered.

An interesting point was brought out regarding the odd claim by James that he went to D.C. to see the zoo. Government prosecutors observed that Baltimore had its own zoo in Druid Hill Park, about two and a half miles from where James lived. The implication was that James really went into D.C. with evil on his mind. Although it really couldn't be proved, police and prosecutors were somewhat skeptical of James's tale about playing tourist at the White House and Navy Yard. A hike from the Navy Yard to the National Zoo via the White House to the murder site is roughly eight miles. While he easily could have covered that much ground between his likely morning arrival and the murder, it does seem like an awfully long distance to walk on a lark. Locating the 7:23 a.m. train from Baltimore was critical, for if he didn't arrive in D.C. until 1:30 p.m., as originally thought, then it would have been a very tight timetable to make his wanderings before the crime. By insisting that he arrived in D.C. early in the morning, he was hurting his case rather than helping it.

Investigators eventually found two witnesses who provided a positive identification of James as someone they saw near the murder scene. One of the witnesses, eventually identified as Trudie Mae Stancil, had her identity and evidence concealed by the police, and the name of the other witness was never disclosed. Another piece of evidence placing James near the crime scene was part of his confession where he mentioned seeing a man mowing his lawn shortly after James left the murder site. He described the man's clothing in some detail, and police canvassed the neighborhood to see if anyone matched his description. They were able to locate a man who reported mowing his lawn at the time in question, wearing the clothes described by James. It was strongly suggestive that James was telling the truth in at least parts of his confession. Detectives also found a publicly unnamed man and woman who testified that they saw James at the zoo and identified him when shown a picture by police. Additionally, a railroad brakeman told coworkers and later police that he thought he saw James at the Anacostia freight yard on the day of the murder.

The grand jury issued an indictment for first-degree murder on July 19 but did not issue an indictment for rape. U.S. attorney George Fay declined to comment on the lack of a rape charge, but presumably the lack of a fully completed or conventional rape left the grand jury in doubt as to whether the charge could be sustained by the medical evidence. Although of course not dealing directly with the Bardwell murder, the trial for the death of Marsha Brill offered a preview of what a trial for the D.C. crime might look like. In particular, the inevitable debate about James's sanity would be significant. James did not take the stand in the Baltimore trial and presumably would have done the same in D.C. Perhaps not surprisingly, the *Afro American* was the only paper to express doubt as to James's guilt after the grand jury. While right to be suspicious of a circumstance that might allow the police to clear an unsolved murder, the writer's suspicions were ultimately just that, suspicions, and dubious assertions, such as the claim that white people wouldn't be able to recognize a Black man they had previously seen.

Indicted in the Baltimore case on July 9, James pleaded not guilty by reason of insanity in both the Brill murder and the separate June 15 rape case. By now he was represented by William Murphy, also Black, although it wasn't clear who was footing the bill. Murphy requested three weeks to prepare for the case and asked for a trial by judge rather than a jury trial. Murphy soon had assistance, as he requested that Charles Houston, who we met in the chapter defending Julius Fisher, join him as co-counsel, and Houston agreed. Houston made sure to tell the press that he was acting in a personal capacity and was not representing the NAACP, which undoubtedly did not want to be associated with a child-killer whose guilt was never really in doubt.

The trial was postponed until September 20 after Murphy said that he needed more time to investigate, and an important witness would not be available on the original trial date. It was still a rapid path to trial, even by the standards of 1948. As the trial began, not surprisingly, Murphy and Houston tried to have James's confession barred from the trial, but they were unsuccessful, and Judge Herman Moser admitted it into evidence. They argued that the confession was taken under duress and accused the police of falsely promising James that he would be admitted to a mental institution if he confessed. Police officers on the stand denied that they made this promise. The defense did succeed with a motion that all witnesses were to be barred from the trial until they testified. Barbara Sapperstein was brought on the stand. She and her brother Alan had viewed two lineups with James in them but didn't make a positive identification. On the stand, Barbara said that James resembled the man who attacked Marsha and correctly noted that while James now wore a beard, he had not had one at the time of the murder. When shown a set of clothes taken from James's home, she agreed that the killer wore similar clothes. Another witness saw him walking near the murder site on July 6, whittling a stick with a long knife and wearing blue dungarees. Saying the man she saw resembled Joe Louis, she pointed out James in the courtroom as the man she saw. (In his confession, James indeed stated that he was whittling a stick that day.) Another witness definitively identified the bloodstained dungaree pants found at James's house as belonging to him, as she was the one who gave them to him when she hired him for a painting job. The evidence of his guilt was quite simply overwhelming.

In the most relevant preview of what might happen in a trial for Bardwell's death, five psychiatrists debated James's sanity. Per Maryland law, sanity meant that the accused "knew the difference between right and wrong and the nature and consequences of his act as applied to himself." Dr. Manfred Guttmacher testified for the prosecution and said that James had a severe mental disorder and made things up while crudely trying to play crazy, but he knew right from wrong. Guttmacher described James as malingering in a "stupid, psychopathic way," which partially explained why some parts of his story were clearly not true while others clearly were. He added that James was an "extremely difficult person to examine because of the unreliability and inconsistency of his answers." James told Guttmacher of his childhood, and the psychiatrist was intrigued by his story of being continually bullied and beaten by a group of fifteen girls at school. In fact, James said that this was the reason he quit school, not that he couldn't intellectually handle it. He added that because of these attacks, "I said to myself, I hate all women," and Guttmacher agreed that his hatred of women might have its roots in these incidents. Additionally, he referenced the "physical sexual deformity" mentioned earlier that he thought might "play a very important part in the patient's reaction to women and to sexual matters."

Dr. J.D.N. Cushing and Dr. Irving Spear gave similar testimony for the prosecution and made clear their opinion that James was legally sane. Spear commented that his reported mental age of eleven was below normal but "average for his race and opportunities," which prompted a question from

Houston as to what race had to do with it. Spear replied that "unfortunately, certain races don't have the same opportunities and conditions as others," and this seems to have been one of the few times when race came up in the case. The defense brought Dr. Philip Lerner and Dr. Herbert Schoenrich to provide competing testimony. They insisted that James was not sane and nothing he said could be relied on. Dr. Philip Lerner gave his estimate of James's intellectual age as just under that of a ten-year-old. They had an uphill task to prove that James didn't know what he was doing was wrong, given that he hid the murder weapon and told lies to the police to try to cover his tracks. Schoenrich rather incredibly offered up a diagnosis of "schizophrenia, unclassified, with paranoid trends" based almost solely on a Rorschach test that he administered; most modern psychiatrists place little or no scientific validity in Rorschach tests.

The only other defense witnesses were James's mother, Bessie, and a sister, Marie, who both gave some details on his life. His mother said that her husband died when Eugene was young and that her son quit school when he was fourteen and couldn't get past fourth grade. (James earlier told police that he was in school through fifth grade and could read and write.) She also said that he had been hit in the head with a loaded (i.e. weighted) cane when he was eleven during a fight and had never been normal since then. Bessie and Marie gave some testimony about James's whereabouts on July 6 and the clothes he was wearing, none of which particularly helped his case. They claimed that he was at their house around noon, but given the vagueness of their statements and the distance from their house to the murder scene, it wasn't much of an alibi even if true. Moreover, police produced a statement signed by Bessie that contained different information about her son's whereabouts on July 6. She lamely said that she didn't write it but signed it after a policeman read it to her, not explaining why she signed it if it wasn't accurate.

All in all, the defense had little to work with, and the *Washington Post* called Houston's and Murphy's defense a "brilliant but foredoomed attempt." In closing arguments, Houston could only argue that James did not have the mental capacity for premeditation and that he should be convicted in the second degree. He was not successful, and Judge Moser took little time on September 22 to convict James of murder in the first degree for the death of Marsha Brill. Sentencing was deferred pending an unsuccessful appeal motion; even though James refused to sign the paperwork to file any appeals, Moser authorized his defense team to sign the papers for him. Moser did compliment Houston, albeit with a slightly patronizing air, saying that he was "as good a counselor as has ever been heard in this court." After the Supreme Bench of Baltimore declined to hear the case on November 7, James was back in front of Judge Moser for sentencing on November 10. Murphy made a last, desperate plea to save James's life, saying that he was a "sick man" and could usefully be studied by psychiatrists. With a first-degree murder conviction, Judge Moser had two options: life imprisonment or death. Moser went with death, which in Maryland meant hanging. He stressed that James knew the difference between right and wrong, and he observed that James possessed "senseless hostility toward immature females" that would never be cured. James was expressionless throughout the sentencing, just as he had been throughout the trial. Houston and Murphy appealed the sentence, telling the Court of Appeals that James's long confinement and questioning on July 8 was "an attack on the human mind more sinister than the use of force," but the jurists unanimously rejected this claim. They noted that any interrogation is going to rely on psychological pressure to some extent, and the defense had not proved that it crossed the line into psychological torture. Attempts several months later to have the Maryland governor commute the sentence were likewise useless.

The charges for the June 15 rape and robbery were dropped by the State of Maryland following his death sentence, and likewise, from the moment he was indicted for Brill's murder, there was little expectation that he would ever face justice for Carol Bardwell's murder. The guilt in the Brill case was so overwhelming that it would have been remarkable if he was acquitted. Had he only been convicted of second-degree murder, then the decision would have been made as to whether to pursue the D.C. case. As it stood, his death sentence meant that there would have been no benefit to taxpayers to finance a prosecution for Bardwell's murder. Carol's parents never publicly stated whether they wished for whatever closure a trial and conviction might bring. The outcome of a trial for Carol's murder almost certainly would have been very similar to what actually happened in Baltimore. Without the full evidence, particularly the eyewitnesses who allegedly saw James in Rock Creek Park and the zoo, being aired in a trial, it's difficult to say how solid the prosecution's case would have been. However, given the totality of the available evidence, there seems to be little reason to doubt James's guilt in the Bardwell murder. Following the Brill trial, Detective Murray told the press that his department would carry the Bardwell case as "closed with indictment." Murray earlier stated that "we are convinced we have the right man," and Police Chief Barrett publicly said that there was enough evidence to get a conviction.

Justice moved swiftly in those days, and on August 12, 1949, Eugene James met his fate. He had no visitors on his last day of life other than the prison chaplain. Up to twenty-five visitors were allowed to attend executions, and eighteen citizens of Baltimore opted to watch the events of that night for their own inscrutable reasons. Two chaplains, a doctor and four reporters were also present. The group was led into the whitewashed execution room, created by knocking out the walls and ceilings of several old cells, resulting in a long, narrow room with a tall ceiling to accommodate the steel platform that composed the gallows. At midnight, another man, guilty of murdering his girlfriend in a rage, preceded James on the gallows. As soon as he was pronounced dead and removed, James was brought in at 12:15 a.m. Brave only when attacking defenseless young girls, James was in a state of near collapse and had to be supported all the way to the gallows. Prison staff moved quickly and bound his arms and legs, and at exactly 12:21 a.m., he dropped below the trapdoor. His death was a grim affair; the noose slipped, and his neck did not break. He visibly writhed and could be heard to cry out in pain. Two guards rushed to hold his legs while a prison doctor administered a morphine injection to reduce his suffering, yet James managed to break one arm loose from his bindings and reach toward the noose before going limp and expiring after nearly fifteen minutes of struggling. A priest offered a blessing over the dead man, and the body was removed. Prison staff were left to embarrassedly report that this was the first botched execution in twenty years. While few people likely felt much displeasure at James's painful end, the bungled execution did contribute to Maryland's decision to switch to the gas chamber method several years later. Regardless, James's unpleasant end meant that there was one less evil man to prey on the children of the capital area.

CHAPTER 6
THE VALUE OF A LIFE

There are occasions when the justice system is in a position to place a specific value on a human life, and the valuations often are not attractive. Such was the case in February 1951. Just before 8:00 a.m. on February 26, a burly man walked into the Fifth Precinct police station and announced, "I beat my wife last night and I can't wake her up." Police privates Arthur Boggs and Lindon Coppage rushed to the man's home at 318 11ᵗʰ Street SE, and he pointed them toward a nude woman lying in bed, covered by a sheet up to her chin. A few steps away was a crib with an infant sleeping peacefully, and in the next room, two other young boys lay asleep; the two boys soon awoke, and Coppage shielded them from the sight of their mother's body. The officers began to unravel the tale; the man was thirty-five-year-old Stanley Szary, a U.S. Air Force master sergeant stationed at Bolling Air Force Base. The woman lying in bed was his wife, Wilma, thirty-six, described as a "statuesque blonde." A note on the dining room table explained most of the story:

> *To whom it may concern: Last night unwittingly I killed my wife. She went out on me. Don't know where she went. But she sure was stinko. I only meant to straighten her out but I must have been too rough with her.*
>
> *Please have some one take care of the boys. Dad's name and address is Antoni Szary, Box 194, Jacobs Creek, Pa.*
>
> *Just can't go on like this. But guess I am the one to blame.*

Szary filled in the gaps. On the previous evening, Saturday the twenty-fifth, he was upstairs in their home, drinking whiskey and listening to the radio, when around 7:00 or 7:30 p.m. Wilma called upstairs that she was going shopping at a local five-and-ten-cent store. However, Wilma did not return until shortly before midnight, and Stanley "flew into a rage" and accused his wife of neglecting their children, four-year-old Stanley Jr., two-year-old William and three-month-old Nicholas. Berating her for being a "bad wife," he lashed out violently. He told the investigating officers he didn't know how many times he hit his wife, but his hands were "sore, hurt and were swollen so I must have hit her a lot more than I thought." When he realized that she had gone unconscious under his beating, he undressed her and put her into bed, then tossed her bloodstained dress and underwear into the bathtub. He then laid down next to her in bed and went to sleep for several hours; when he awoke, he called her name and tried to shake her awake. It dawned on him that his wife would never awaken, and after covering her body with a sheet, he composed the note that officers found on the table.

After checking that his children were in bed, he claimed to the officers that he planned to shoot himself with his .38-caliber pistol and drove around in the family car for several hours but "lost his nerve." He placed a second note in the car's glovebox that simply said, "Go to 318 Eleventh St. SE," but when he found he couldn't go through with his suicide, he placed the pistol in the glovebox and turned himself in at the police station. In later testimony, a neighbor "partially refuted" Szary's story, according to police, saying that after Wilma returned from the five-and-ten-cent store, he sent her out to buy a fifth of whiskey for him. It was her lateness from this errand that infuriated him. At about 1:00 a.m., the neighbor and his daughter thought they heard the Szary children crying and Wilma saying something in a loud voice. Stanley alleged that Wilma was imbibing that night as well, hence the "stinko" comment in his note, but of course the full truth can't be known, nor should it have been particularly relevant. The influence of alcohol was clear regardless, as police found "several whiskey bottles, empty and partially filled," in the house. Authorities arrived to take baby Nicholas to Gallinger Hospital and the two other boys to the Industrial School Annex until relatives could arrive to take them in. Szary's parents in Pittsburgh would shortly take the children into their care.

At the coroner's jury held at the District Morgue, Szary, stocky at five feet, six inches tall and 187 pounds, appeared "dejected, hardly able to talk" and was "shaking visibly" with his head in his hands. Without a lawyer present, he began to answer questions asked of him, but when told they could be

The house where Wilma Szary was murdered still stands in a pleasant residential neighborhood. It is the house between the light pole and the large tree. *Author's collection.*

used against him in a court of law, he "mumbled his refusal" to testify and did not take the stand. He acted like a man "in a trance" but snapped to attention whenever Coroner A. Magruder MacDonald asked him a question. He awaited the inevitable verdict, which took only ten minutes to arrive. The graphic coroner's report left no doubt that Stanley would be held for grand jury action. Deputy Coroner Richard Rosenberg testified that Wilma died from a cerebral hemorrhage, evidenced by a bloody nose, and a ruptured liver and kidney. She also suffered ten broken ribs with a mass of bruises across her entire face and body. Policeman Boggs, one of those who responded to the scene, later testified that there was no part of Wilma's body that he saw unmarked by violence. In his words, the beating was "the worst I've ever seen."

Szary's indictment for second-degree murder followed on March 19; his journey through the legal system would prove to be a short one. In another example of the small world of the D.C. legal community, Szary retained

Burly Stanley Szary is taken into custody for his wife's murder. *Courtesy of AP Wirephoto.*

Charles Ford as his attorney, the same lawyer who had successfully defended "Dutch" Kappel in 1935. On June 4, assistant United States attorney William Arnold made the recommendation for a plea deal to Judge Henry Schweinhaut; Szary agreed to plead guilty to the lesser charge of manslaughter, which held a maximum penalty of five to fifteen years in prison. He was released on $5,000 bond while awaiting sentencing, which occurred on June 29.

Szary's military record would weigh heavily in his favor as Judge Schweinhaut decided his sentence. Originally from western Pennsylvania, the master sergeant had over a decade of service behind him, having enlisted prior to the outbreak of World War II in what was then the U.S. Army Air Corps. He served honorably as an aircraft mechanic throughout the war. Apparently, he spent most of the war stateside but did serve in the Philippines for six months at the tail end of the war, returning home just before Christmas 1945. He emerged from the war with awards including the Good Conduct Medal, Meritorious Unit Citation, Asiatic Pacific Theater ribbon, American Defense Service Medal and Philippines Liberation ribbon. He reenlisted in early 1946 at Barksdale Field in Shreveport, Louisiana. This was a fateful posting, as there he met and married Wilma, a native of Mississippi who had gone to high school in Shreveport and lived there for a number of years. She had a daughter from a previous marriage, and at least at some point, Szary helped care for and support this stepchild. Stationed at Bolling Field since June 1946, he worked in the engineering section of the 1111th Special Air Mission Squadron. His commander and other superior officers "stood by him" during the episode. His line chief told a reporter that Szary was "one of the best men I had. He kept his aircraft in perfect shape. I'd say he was very stable, very conscientious." The line chief then thought for a few seconds and added, "There was one thing, though. He always kept to himself. Nobody knew him very well."

On the twenty-ninth, Szary stood in court with his sister Sophia for support. There, Judge Schweinhaut announced his rather incredible sentencing decision: Szary would pay a fine of $1,000. He would be placed in jail only until he paid his fine, and then he would be a free man. That would prove not to be an issue; attorney Ford had the $1,000 in hand, ready to pay the fine. Schweinhaut justified this sentence on the grounds that both Szary and his wife had been drinking heavily that night, he had a "perfect record" in the military and "the slaying was apparently unintentional." In a curious bit of logic, Schweinhaut also gave weight to the fact that the children needed an appropriate person to take care of them, regardless of the fact that the parent in question had murdered the other. A newspaper article reporting the sentence also noted, without comment, that in the past several days a burglar who stole $4,700 in jewels to feed his drug habit had been sentenced to one to five years' incarceration, two men got five to fifteen years for robbing and beating a man and a man was given ten to thirty years for second-degree murder in a stabbing case.

The decision did not escape censure, and in September, Wilma's hometown representative in Congress, Overton Brooks of Louisiana, made a speech on the matter in Congress, saying that he "wanted to point out the judicial value placed upon human life by the District bench in Washington, D.C." He archly noted that regarding assistant U.S. attorney Arnold, "someone else must have thought…[he] did a good job" since he had been promoted to an attorney position in the Justice Department Claims division. Brooks asked for Congress to look into the matter. Queried for comment by the media, Arnold said that the charge was reduced "because of the difficulties presented in getting a murder conviction" due to Szary's confession as being the main evidence. In fact, he said there was "no chance" of a murder conviction because "both were drunk" and that "we were lucky" to get any conviction. He defensively added that the sentence was "entirely the responsibility of the court" and the judge could have given him fifteen years in prison if he wanted to. Brooks also highlighted the fact that Szary was allowed to return to duty after paying his fine as though nothing had happened, which prompted a rather sarcastic statement by a Bolling public affairs officer that double jeopardy prevented the U.S. Air Force from court-martialing Szary on the same charge and that "even the Congressman should know about double jeopardy."

Adding a final insult, Szary raised the money to pay the fine by selling property jointly belonging to him and the wife he had just killed. During the legal proceedings, two sons went to live with his sister in Pennsylvania and the third with his brother in Chicago, but he retained custody of the children. This occurred even though Wilma's parents, Mr. and Mrs. W.D.

Daniels of Shreveport, wanted the children and a child welfare investigation found them to be qualified to raise them. When they approached Arnold about custody, he informed them that his office could do nothing about it since custody was a civil matter. Wilma's body was returned to Shreveport for burial, where her modest grave incorrectly gives March 2 as the date of death.

At first it appeared that Szary would be able to resume his U.S. Air Force career as if nothing happened, for he remained on active duty status throughout the case and initially returned to his position at Bolling after paying his fine. But the pressure brought by Representative Brooks and Wilma's family eventually bore fruit. Wilma's uncle Thomas wrote directly to Lieutenant General Hoyt Vandenberg, pointedly asking, "Will you kindly advise me what the USAF policy is in dealing with enlisted personnel who commit murder away from their base?" After relating Szary's story, he noted that Bolling officials "did not do a thing," but his understanding was that it "would have been quite different" at Barksdale Air Force Base. The letter was referred to Brigadier General Albert Kuhfeld, assistant judge advocate general, who wrote back on November 21 saying that it would be illegal to court-martial Szary for an offense he had been convicted of in federal court. However, Kuhfeld did reveal that the U.S. Air Force discharged Szary on November 5 with a provision that he was barred from reenlisting. Presumably, the U.S. Air Force had exercised its ability to administratively discharge service members on grounds of unacceptable character or morals. After he was discharged, Szary returned to Pennsylvania and began a second career as a steelworker in Pittsburgh before dying in 2001. His obituary carries a line eerie and ironic to those who know about the man's life: "He was preceded in death by his wife, Wilma Daniels Szary."

CHAPTER 7

A REVOLUTION IN THE MIND

Onie Belle Mullis was a woman determined to keep her family together. In April 1958, the attractive twenty-five-year-old would prove to just what lengths she was willing to go to do so. Described by friends as a "very sweet person, always pleasant to everyone," she resided at 1111 North Kensington Street in Arlington, Virginia, with her twenty-nine-year-old husband, John, and their eight-year-old daughter Beverley Anne. The two were native North Carolinians who had married nine years earlier when Onie was at the young age of sixteen. (Onie clearly did not have an easy life, as she apparently had a son by another man at age fourteen, who was raised by her family.) After some time in Detroit, they had been living in Arlington for about two years. John worked at the office of the American Federation of State, County and Municipal Employees in D.C. as a refrigeration engineer.

The problem was that Kathryn Joyce, a thirty-year-old clerk-typist formerly of Scranton, Pennsylvania, worked in the same building. She and John Mullis were having a torrid affair that began in February 1957 after he gave her a ride home only two weeks after she started her job. Onie learned of the affair in May 1957 when she saw that her husband had written Joyce's name and number in their telephone directory at home. Her husband claimed that Joyce was a secretary at his company, and he needed to be able to call her for work, but any illusions Onie had were dispelled by July. While Onie was in North Carolina visiting family, John remained in Arlington with Joyce. He not only brought his lover to the Mullis house, but he also called his wife and informed her that he couldn't drive to North Carolina to pick her up because he had no money, presumably having spent it on his mistress. When she managed to return home, Onie was suspicious, for her husband's call to her in North Carolina had been a collect call from a number she didn't recognize. Checking with the phone company, she found that her husband had placed the call from Joyce's residence. In August, Onie and a friend trailed her husband and Joyce from D.C. and saw Joyce draping her arm over John and kissing him. When the lovers chose the rather unusual lover's lane spot of the Arlington Courthouse to park, Onie angrily confronted the pair. She begged John to break off the illicit relationship; he said he would but had no intention of doing so, sometimes going to see Joyce mere minutes after promising to break things off. He later acknowledged that he was with Joyce "every possible chance," sometimes every night, and that they "had relations" in her apartment and "many times" in his car, which he would park "all over the city" for their activities. He later claimed, not very convincingly, that he wanted to leave Joyce, but "I couldn't. I wanted to, but I couldn't." In September, after John claimed that Joyce had quit her job and left town, Onie called the woman to see if that was true, and in response Joyce "just laughed" at her and freely admitted that she'd "been intimate" with John. Onie later said that on one occasion, Joyce told her, "Your husband wants only me. Look at your dishpan hands. You don't even have lipstick on." Despite more promises by her husband to end the affair, it continued, and Onie later claimed that Joyce called her several times to taunt her about the ongoing affair. In February 1958, Onie followed the pair to Joyce's apartment and found them parked in front of it. Finding them in a compromising position, another argument followed. At home, her husband said he wanted to take a walk to cool off and didn't show up for three days!

Amid all of this drama, on Saturday, April 26, Onie and John enjoyed a rare night out, leaving their daughter with relatives while the pair had a steak supper with another couple. Upon their return between 6:00 and 6:30 p.m., while Onie was changing clothes, the mood soon changed when John announced that he needed to go into work and departed in the family car. Having no doubt where he was really headed, Onie pondered the matter, borrowed a car from a neighbor and went off in pursuit, with an odd item in her purse. Several weeks earlier, John Mullis had made what proved to be an unfortunate choice of gift when he presented Onie with a twelve-inch "imitation Japanese samurai sword letter opener." Onie later insisted she had been carrying the letter opener around in her purse that entire time. Obviously knowing where Joyce lived, she headed to Joyce's residence at 3400 25th Street SE, a fourteen- to fifteen-mile drive depending on the precise route.

Pulling up in front of Joyce's apartment around 9:30 p.m., Onie found the two of them in the family's car, parked in front of the residence. John was apparently asleep while Joyce's head rested on his shoulder. In fact, John later admitted that after meeting Joyce in front of her apartment, the two were "making love" in his car when he saw his wife drive up. He pretended to be asleep, but the understandably agitated Onie opened the car door and slapped John awake. She later claimed she simply wanted to "talk things over" and even more unbelievably said that she asked Joyce to hash things out over a cup of coffee. Her husband pushed her back into the borrowed car while hitting and choking her, got into the driver's seat and began to drive his wife home. During their argument, John struck Onie again as he made a left onto Savannah Street and stopped the car after traveling only a short distance, short enough that Joyce quickly caught up on foot.

The bickering couple got out of the car just before the intersection of 24th Street and Savannah, and Joyce joined the now-violent altercation, hitting and scratching Onie. Reaching into her purse, Onie pulled out the samurai sword letter opener and plunged it into Joyce, who turned and fled down the street. John saw the flash of the blade and then saw blood. Stunned, he later said he "hollered" for an ambulance. Now worked into a frenzy (John later said she was screaming and "acting like a nut"), Onie pursued and kept stabbing her victim as she alternately collapsed, got up, ran and collapsed again for a distance that police later measured at precisely sixty-four yards. When it was all over, Kathryn Joyce was dead from eleven stab wounds: five

Kathryn Joyce's apartment overlooks the spot where Onie Mullis confronted her cheating husband (in the immediate foreground). *Author's collection.*

Here Onie Mullis attacked Kathryn Joyce, chasing her down the sidewalk to the left while stabbing her. *Author's collection.*

in the chest, five in the back and one in the throat. Later, it was determined that five of the wounds were potentially fatal. The last blow was delivered while Joyce lay on the ground. In the fracas, John Mullis received superficial cuts to his leg and chest. Onie did not emerge unscathed either; her torn and bloody clothing bore evidence of several cuts, and two of her teeth were knocked loose.

Police private Robert LaBossiere responded to the scene and later said that Onie was "not normal" when he arrived and was "screaming and hysterical." As the officer approached her, she pointed to John Mullis and sobbed, "Get him away from here, or I'll kill him too." Police private Betty Everhart was soon sent to the scene and spoke to Onie, presumably with the thought that she would open up to a female officer. She apparently did, declaring, "I killed the bitch. I hope she dies." Not surprisingly, Mullis would later deny making these statements to police. In addition, she allegedly said that she put the letter opener in her purse that night "because she anticipated trouble," obviously suggesting premeditation. (Regarding that trouble, a newspaper noted wryly, "she found it.")

Kathryn Joyce's body was returned to Dunmore, Pennsylvania, for burial, and like so many cases, the focus shifted entirely to the killer. While Joyce may have made questionable decisions in romance, she was no doubt mourned by her family back home, but she remains an enigma to us. Virtually no personal information was ever given about her in the press. A coroner's inquest met on April 29, and John refused to testify against his wife, saying he would do whatever he could to help her avoid a conviction. Regardless, grand jury action followed the inquest, and a second-degree murder charge resulted. On May 2, authorities released Onie Mullis on $5,000 bond given that she had no prior record and a psychiatrist said she was not a threat. An assistant U.S. attorney with the wonderfully literary name of Lewis Carroll argued against the bond being granted but was unsuccessful. Members of the Mullis family rushed to Arlington, and John's mother, Minnie, tried to defend the rapidly tarnishing image of John Mullis, saying that after the killing he "sobbed out how much his wife meant to him." She added that the family was "very clannish" and, in trying to explain Onie's actions, said that "I just guess she loved him too much."

Onie was defended by James Laughlin, aided by attorney Albert Ahern Jr., at her trial that began on September 17 following jury selection. Seven men and five women were selected after half a dozen others were excused for sitting on another recent trial that dealt with sanity issues, and fifteen challenges were used. The concerns over bias regarding sanity would soon become apparent. The defense strategy was unsurprising: Onie Mullis was temporarily insane and not in control of her faculties during the killing. It was a classic defense for cases like this. Laughlin placed her period of insanity as a short time of five to twenty minutes. Judge Henry Schweinhaut, the same man who had fined Stanley Szary $1,000 for killing his wife, presided over the case. Assistant U.S. attorney Victor Caputy prosecuted for the government. Those following the case would soon be able to see if attitudes toward wronged spouses had changed since Robert Miller's trial in 1944 or whether Onie's gender would affect the case.

The defense brought psychiatrist Dr. Robert Odenwald, described by a reporter as having a "large briefcase and thick German accent," to the stand. Odenwald testified that based on several examinations of Onie, he concluded that she had a "revolution in the mind" and suffered from a "psychotic disarrangement" when she confronted Kathryn Joyce. As a result, she could not control her actions. He examined her four times between May and September and said that she was clear in answering most questions but became "confused" when asked about the stabbing. Not surprisingly, the government brought their own psychiatrist, Dr. Albert Marland (who you may remember from the 1944 Miller trial), and he testified that generally "emotional experiences do not lead to temporary insanity." Caputy used a familiar tactic to ask him a "four-minute-long hypothetical question" to reinforce this point that Mullis was not suffering from temporary insanity. The jury would have to decide which expert to believe.

Bringing another literary namesake into the case, Kathryn Joyce's brother James appeared as a witness and created a bit of drama. He testified that John Mullis spoke of marriage half a dozen times to his sister during their year-long relationship and said that he was long-separated from his wife and preparing to divorce her. (John Mullis testified that he spoke about divorce to people who knew about the affair to lessen their disapproval but didn't intend to go through with one.) According to James Joyce, Mullis talked of buying a home and furniture for the two. When Mullis followed him on the witness stand, Joyce took exception when he said that he and Kathryn spent several days at her mother's apartment, "with Mr. Joyce sleeping in another bedroom." Also upset by a story from Mullis that claimed James was present on an occasion when Onie Mullis surprised the cheating couple in a car, James shouted out, "That's a lie!" and Judge Schweinhaut ordered him out of the courtroom. Mullis's attorney Laughlin asked for a mistrial but was refused. Mullis, "testifying laconically," denied discussing marriage but admitted that he had seen Joyce nearly every night for a year. He explained that his wife was "flawless" and that he promised her multiple times to stop seeing Joyce but kept going back to spend "practically everything I made" on alcohol and motel rooms. He stated that Onie was "a good girl.…We never argued.…She never lost her temper." He added that he married her when she was "just a child.… She never knew any other man." He had no problem admitting all the details of the affair and acknowledged that some months he spent up to $470 of his $500 salary on Joyce, blowing $40 to $50 each date night. On one occasion, Onie gave him $20 to go to the drugstore to buy medicine for their daughter, and he brushed off the errand to go out with Joyce, money in hand.

Onie's injuries that night were also disputed, as the defense pointed to her torn and bloody clothing and a medical report that said she suffered several cuts and two loose teeth. Defense attorney Laughlin dramatically held Onie's bra in front of the jury, showing them that there was blood on both sides of it. He also pointed to her torn dress to show that she was in a knock-down fight. Conversely, police testified that she told them Joyce "had not laid her hands upon her," in contradiction of her current statement that Joyce scratched, choked and beat her.

Onie sobbed on the stand and "time and again" answered, "I don't recall" when questioned by prosecutor Caputy. He rapidly asked her questions, and her voice became "tinged with anger" as she answered. In her telling, she claimed she wasn't angry when she left her home to look for her husband. When asked if seeing Joyce's head on her husband's shoulder agitated her, she acknowledged that it "would excite any woman." She claimed she had no memory of stabbing Joyce but had a vague recollection that she "stabbed somebody." However, she thought it was her husband. When Caputy asked whether she remembered telling police that Joyce was on the ground the last time she was stabbed, she gave her favored "I don't remember" response. Caputy dramatically acted out her stabbing attack on Joyce, but it did not faze Onie, and she denied telling police that she chased down Joyce. She also denied that she told police that she put the letter opener in her purse that night "because she anticipated trouble" and insisted that it had been in her purse for weeks. She not surprisingly also denied telling police that night that she was "very sorry.…I shouldn't have hurt her.…She didn't do anything.… All she was doing was trying to stop us from fighting."

Caputy gave a fifty-minute closing argument after five days of testimony, accusing Mullis of "coldly forgetting" events. He added that she remembered events up until they could be "detrimental to her," and then her amnesia conveniently kicked in. Caputy ridiculed Mullis's tears on the stand, asking, "Did she shed a tear for Kathryn Joyce?" He acknowledged that her husband was "steeped in sin and callous in conscience" but wanted the jury to focus on her mental state. In his closing, defense attorney Laughlin pursued an emotional tack for an hour and asked the jury to think of the Mullises' daughter before locking up her mother. The only time Onie cried during the trial was at this mention of her daughter. He added that there was "constant taunting" from Joyce and that "this husband led Miss Joyce through the paths of debauchery, but she was asking for exactly what happened." Laughlin asked jurors if they would have reacted differently, and one suspects this was the real thrust of his defense strategy, masked by a convenient temporary insanity defense. He did add that John Mullis was also to blame, noting that women have been stoned for immorality, but "I never heard of this happening to a man." Following the closing arguments, Judge Schweinhaut gave the jury an hour and a half worth of instructions and told them that they could find Onie guilty of murder, guilty of manslaughter, not guilty or not guilty by reason of insanity.

On September 25, after three hours of deliberation, the jury announced their verdict: not guilty by reason of insanity. Onie was nervous and wringing her hands, and when the verdict was announced, she slumped down and dropped her head in relief. The temporary insanity defense had worked, although whether the jury truly believed it or just believed a homewrecker had gotten what she deserved can never really be known. But Onie Mullis wasn't free just yet, as under D.C. law, people receiving this verdict had to stay at St. Elizabeth's Hospital for evaluation until the superintendent could certify their sanity.

Onie Mullis spent several months at sprawling St. Elizabeth's Hospital as her mental state was decided by medical and legal figures. *Courtesy of the Library of Congress.*

Laughlin and Ahern said they would seek her release within a week, but the superintendent, Dr. Winfred Overholser (the deceased Dr. Lind's boss), said six months were needed to assess her. Laughlin intended to use a petition for a writ of habeas corpus to gain an immediate release, but a recent court case made that unlikely. Katharine Haynes had killed her husband's mistress in a similar case a few years earlier and was released in December 1955 after forty-three days of observation. In making the petition, attorneys Laughlin and Ahern said that when Mullis was committed to St. Elizabeth's the week before, the psychiatrist who examined her upon entry "expressed amazement" that she was committed at all. The crux of their argument was that the 1955 law in question that required commitment applied only to long-duration insanity, not temporary insanity. After several weeks of legal back and forth, a judge approved the defense's request for a hearing on the issue of Onie's sanity.

However, at that October 18 hearing, Judge Alexander Holtzoff denied her release, upholding the need for the certification of sanity. Superintendent Overholser and another doctor said two or three more months were needed to evaluate Mullis. It in fact would be longer than that, but on April 16, 1959, Judge F. Dickinson Letts ordered her conditional release on a recommendation from prosecutor Caputy after Dr. Overholser certified that she would not "in the reasonably foreseeable future be dangerous to herself" or others and that she had "not shown evidence of mental illness." Given that Caputy had insisted all along that there was nothing mentally wrong with Onie, he didn't have much choice other than to agree that there was no reason to keep her at St. Elizabeth's. Mullis would have to periodically visit the hospital for interviews, and her family would submit reports as to her mental status.

Following her release, a no doubt relieved Onie Mullis said she did not plan to go back to her husband but would take her daughter to live with her mother in Roanoke Rapids. Onie did in fact make the right decision and divorce the sleazy John Mullis, with their divorce finalized in August 1961. John later remarried and, perhaps not surprisingly, divorced again before he died in 1991. Sadly, Onie would not have long to enjoy herself, as in August 1962, she was killed in a car accident while driving late at night on Highway 301 south of Emporia, Virginia. Her gravestone in Roanoke Rapids bears a simple but no doubt heartfelt sentiment: "We Miss Your Smile."

BIBLIOGRAPHY

Chapter 1

Commonwealth of Virginia. Death certificate for William H. Reaguer, February 26, 1945. Ancestry.com.

Free Lance-Star (Fredericksburg, VA). "Cousin on Stand in Reaguer Trial." April 21, 1936.

———. "Reaguer Unsound Night of Murder." April 22, 1936.

———. "Says Undertaker Threatened Bride." October 15, 1935.

Northern Virginia Daily. "Reaguer Gave Wife Presents, Wood Testifies." April 22, 1936.

———. "Sordid Romance Revealed in Culpeper Bride Slaying." October 16, 1935.

Orange [VA] Review. "Reaguer Is Given Sentence of Life: Mercy Plea Fails." May 14, 1936.

Richmond [VA] News Leader. "Charters." July 2, 1937.

———. "Mrs. Bessie M. Reaguer." December 30, 1936.

Roanoke [VA] Times. "William Earle Reaguer." September 1, 1934.

Tarver, William. "Doctor Says Reaguer Told Him Girl Killed Self in Suicide Pact." April 27, 1936.

———. "Girls' Detention by Reaguer Told." *Washington Evening Star*, April 21, 1936.

———. "Mrs. Wood Called On Reaguer, Says Witness in Trial." April 24, 1936.

———. "Parents of Girls Kept Off Reaguer Jury by Defense." *Washington Evening Star*, April 20, 1936.

———. "Reaguer Changed in Recent Years, Witnesses Aver." April 23, 1936.

———. "Reaguer Defense Offers Final Pleas as Case Moves to Jury." April 30, 1936.

———. "Reaguer Evidence All Before Jury; Insanity Scouted." April 29, 1936.

———. "Reaguer Fear of Chair Shown in Implements for Suicide." May 2, 1936.

———. "Reaguer Insane, Alienist Asserts as Defense Rests." April 28, 1936.

———. "Reaguer Is Found Guilty of Murder in Second Degree." May 1, 1936.

———. "U.S. Rests Case as Reaguer Sobs." April 22, 1936.

Times-News (Hendersonville, NC). "Hold Undertaker in Murder Case." October 16, 1935.

Virginia Star (Culpeper, VA). "W.H. Reaguer." March 1, 1945.

Washington Daily News. "Bride Murdered in Local Hotel." October 12, 1935.

———. "Bride's Cousin Tells of Reaguer's Effort to 'Get Rid of Her.'" April 21, 1936.

———. "Inquest Gets Details of Bride's Slaying." October 15, 1935.

———. "Mrs. Wood Visited Reaguer Day Before Death, Witness Says." April 24, 1936.

———. "Reaguer Guilty; Escapes Chair." May 1, 1936.

———. "Reaguer's Account of 'Death Pact' Told by Doctor in Court." April 27, 1936.

Washington Evening Star. "Father of 2 Held after Slaying of Virginian's Bride." October 12, 1935.

———. "Inquest Starts in Bride's Death." October 15, 1935.

———. "Plan Third Court for Crime Cases." April 13, 1936.

———. "Probe Tomorrow in Killing of Bride." October 14, 1935.

———. "Reaguer Charged with Bride Killing." October 16, 1935.

———. "Reaguer Defense in Final Stages." April 26, 1936.

———. "Reaguer to Begin Life Term Today." May 9, 1936.

———. "Threats to Slain Bride Revealed." October 13, 1935.

———. "Trial of Reaguer Opens Tomorrow." April 19, 1936.

———. "Undertaker Indicted in Slaying." November 6, 1935.

Washington Herald. "Coroner Jury to Sift Murder." October 14, 1935.

———. "Defense Refuses to Call Reaguer." April 26, 1936.

———. "Mad Jealousy Called Motive in Girl Killing." October 13, 1935.

———. "Reaguer Branded 'Dangerous.'" April 28, 1936.

———. "Reaguer Defense Calls Alienists." April 25, 1936.

———. "Reaguer Held to Grand Jury in Girl Killing." October 16, 1935.

———. "Reaguer Is Given Life Sentence." May 9, 1936.

———. "Reaguer Jury Is Locked Up after 7 Hours." May 1, 1936.

———. "Slain Girl's Love Letters Read." April 24, 1936.

———. "Slain Girl's Mate Charges Threat." April 22, 1936.

———. "Slain Girl's Words to Reaguer Denied." April 29, 1936.

———. "Suitor Threatened Death to Bride, 21." April 21, 1936.

———. "Wife Backs Mate in Love Slaying." April 23, 1936.

Washington Post. "Bride's Death Inquiry Will Hear Reaguer." October 14, 1935.

———. "Cousin Details Slaying of Girl in Capital Hotel." April 21, 1936.

———. "Jury May Get Reaguer Case by Tomorrow." April 27, 1936.

———. "Miss Reaguer, of Culpeper, Church Bride." June 24, 1934.

———. "Murder Trial of Undertaker Is Tomorrow." April 19, 1936.

———. "Police Blame Bride Slaying in Hotel Here on Admirer." October 13, 1935.

———. "Reaguer Case May Go to Jury This Afternoon." April 30, 1936.

———. "Reaguer Given Life Sentence in Girl's Death." May 9, 1936.

———. "Reaguer Guilty; Given 20 Years in Girl's Death." May 2, 1936.

———. "Reaguer Happy, Waits Transfer to Lorton Cell." May 3, 1936.

———. "Reaguer Jurors Fail to Agree; Are Locked Up." May 1, 1936.

———. "Reaguer Jury Given Letters of Slain Wife." April 24, 1936.

———. "Reaguer Made Threat on Life, Wood Testifies." April 22, 1936.

———. "Reaguer Sane When He Killed Girl, District Alienist Asserts." April 29, 1936.

———. "Reaguer's Kin Tell of Illness Before Killing." April 23, 1936.

———. "Two Alienists Tell Jurymen Reaguer Insane." April 28, 1936.

———. "Witnesses Tell Jury Reaguer Seemed Insane." April 25, 1936.

Washington Times. "Bride's Death Described by Girl." April 21, 1936.

———. "Defense Rests Case in Reaguer Trial." April 28, 1936.

———. "Final Debate on Reaguer Due Today." April 29, 1936.

———. "Ill Health Defense of Reaguer." April 23, 1936.

———. "Jury Finds Reaguer Guilty." May 1, 1936.

———. "Quiz Reaguer in Slaying of Bride." October 14, 1935.

———. "Reaguer Case Will Reach Jury Today." April 30, 1936.

———. "Reaguer Held for Jury as Murderer." October 16, 1935.

———. "Reaguer Jury Completed." April 20, 1936.

———. "Reaguer Protected Against Suicide Try." May 2, 1936.

———. "Reaguer Resumes Fight for Life Monday in Slaying Trial." April 25, 1936.

———. "Reaguer's Plea of Insanity in Slaying Trial Backed by Witness." April 24, 1936.

———. "Reaguer: Undertaker Accused of Threats." October 15, 1935.

———. "Slain Girl's Parent Buried." April 8, 1936.

———. "Tears Shed by Reaguer at Trial." April 22, 1936.

———. "3 Alienists Quizzed on Reaguer." April 27, 1936.

———. "Young Bride Is Slain in D.C. Hotel." October 12, 1935.

Wentworth, Howard. "Inquest Hears Killing in Hotel Here Described as 'Defense' Act." *Washington Post*, October 16, 1935.

Chapter 2

Gilmore, Eddy. "Phone Girl Shot Dead; 2 D.C. Men Are Held." *Washington Daily News*, November 27, 1935.

Washington Daily News. "Alibi in Phone Girl's Death Aided by Hacker." November 30, 1935.

———. "Hacker Who Carried Kappel to Club on Death Night Sought." November 29, 1935.

———. "Lynch Inquest Jury Views Broken Chair Found Around Body." December 3, 1935.

———. "Police Check Activities of Slain Phone Operator." November 28, 1935.

Washington Evening Star. "'Break' Held Near in Lynch Death; Officers Silent." November 30, 1935.

———. "Coroner's Jury Gets Lynch Case." December 3, 1935.

———. "Costello Is Held in Shooting Here." December 13, 1932.

———. "'Crime' in Question, Pair Are Released." June 14, 1937.

———. "Cullen Released in Lynch Slaying." December 1, 1935.

———. "Death of Grady Held Accidental." November 26, 1928.

———. "District Motorist Gets Three Years." June 11, 1931.

———. "Divorce Is Sought by Kappel's Wife." August 25, 1936.

———. "Fierst Pleads Guilty in $9,400 Holdup." December 15, 1939.

———. "Gold Smuggling Ring Hunt Begins." December 10, 1933.

———. "Grady Death Still Baffles Officials." November 25, 1928.

———. "Indictment Returned in Hold-up of Two That Netted $1,650." December 14, 1938.

———. "Inquest Tomorrow in Lynch Murder." December 2, 1935.

———. "Jewelry Bandit Pleads Larceny." April 24, 1931.

———. "Kappel Case Action Ended after Evidence Is Reviewed." June 28, 1936.

———. "Kappel Case Dropped; Complainant Leaves City." February 27, 1938.

———. "Kappel Files Appeal for Another Trial." April 29, 1939.

———. "Kappel Found Guilty on Robbery Charges." April 26, 1939.

———. "Kappel Indicted on Murder Charge in Phone Girl's Death." January 6, 1936.

———. "Kappel Is Arraigned on Murder Charges." January 10, 1936.

———. "Kappel Is Sentenced from 2 to 8 Years on Robbery Charge." May 5, 1939.

———. "Motion for Mistrial in Kappel Case Denied by Court." April 24, 1939.

———. "Pair Surrenders in Resort Fight." December 23, 1930.

———. "Plan Third Court for Crime Cases." April 13, 1936.

———. "Probe Continues in Lynch Death." December 4, 1935.

———. "Protection Asked by Mrs. Kappel." June 27, 1936.

———. "Revolver Is Tested for Fingerprints in Lynch Death." November 28, 1935.

———. "Shooting Case Dropped." January 12, 1933.

———. "Skylight Death Is Investigated." November 21, 1928.

———. "Slain Woman's Sister Asks Estate Power." December 13, 1935.

———. "Suspected Assailant of Constable Freed." January 26, 1929.

———. "Suspects' Alibis in Lynch Slaying Being Checked." November 29, 1935.

———. "10,000 Bond Fixed in $1,650 Holdup." November 28, 1938.

———. "Two Men Quizzed as Slain Woman Is Found in Home." November 27, 1935.

———. "Two Men Sought in Death Inquiry." November 24, 1928.

———. "Two Women Held as Man Is Shot." December 12, 1932.

Washington Herald. "Alibi Checkup Balks Police in Lynch Death." November 29, 1935.

———. "Coroner's Jury Holds Kappel." December 4, 1935.

———. "Hacker Backs Kappel Alibi in Lynch Murder." November 30, 1935.

————. "Murder of Girl Jails Two Men." November 28, 1935.

Washington Post. "Constable's Action Liberates Suspect." January 26, 1929.

————. "Divorce Is Asked by Wife of Kappel, Freed in Slaying." August 25, 1936.

————. "'Dutch' Kappel Charged with Holdup Here." November 27, 1938.

————. "Grady's Family Plans Further Death Inquiry." November 27, 1928.

————. "Inquest Set Today on Phone Operator." December 3, 1935.

————. "Jury Prepares Lynch Slaying Report Today." December 11, 1935.

————. "Kappel, Companion Freed in Robbery." June 15, 1937.

————. "Kappel Held Slayer of Elizabeth Lynch." December 4, 1935.

————. "Kappel, Jailed 37 Times, Gets 1st Prison Term." April 26, 1939.

————. "Man Freed in Shooting on Victim's Statement." January 12, 1933.

————. "Man's Death Fall Accidental, Belief." November 22, 1928.

————. "Police Brand Lynch Killing Murder Plot." November 29, 1935.

————. "Police Drop Probe of Shooting Riddle." December 13, 1932.

————. "Police Given Rules in Prince George's." June 10, 1931.

————. "Police to Drop Investigation in Kappel Case." June 28, 1936.

————. "Police to Test Alibis of Pair in Lynch Case." November 30, 1935.

————. "Roomer Freed in 1935 Killing of Phone Girl." June 27, 1936.

————. "2 Men Jailed as Police Sift Girl's Slaying." November 28, 1935.

————. "Two More Men Held in Grady Death Inquiry." November 24, 1928.

————. "2 More Seized in Mysterious Fall of Grady." November 26, 1928.

Washington Times. "Alibi Studied in Lynch Killing." November 30, 1935.

————. "Brothers Hurt in Inn Fight Recover." December 23, 1930

————. "'Dutch' Kappel Is Indicted in $1,650 Holdup." December 14, 1938.

————. "Kappel Freed in Two Cases." January 26, 1929.

————. "Lynch Inquest Postponed by Police." November 29, 1935.

————. "Phone Girl Slain in Home." November 27, 1935.

————. "Police Hint Fight Preceded Grady Death." November 24, 1928.

————. "Release of Kappel Probed." June 27, 1936.

————. "Shooting Suspect Gives Up and Claims Innocence." December 13, 1932.

————. "3 Sought in Grady Death." November 23, 1928.

————. "2 Men Grilled in Lynch Case." November 28, 1935.

————. "2 Quizzed in Grady Death." November 26, 1928.

————. "2 Women Held after Shooting at Party." December 12, 1932.

————. "Wife Charges Cruelty by Spouse." August 25, 1936.

Chapter 3

Carper, Elise. "Sailor, First to Reach Car, Halts Suspect." *Washington Post*, February 22, 1944.

Cassini, Austine. "These Charming People." *Washington Times Herald*, March 1, 1944.

Champlain, Helene. "Warned Him Not to See 'That Woman,' Declares Daughter of Slain Psychiatrist." *Washington Post*, February 22, 1944.

Dixon, George. "Lind Gun 'Planted,' Eyewitness Hints at Slaying Inquest." *Washington Times Herald*, February 24, 1944.

———. "Miller Asks to Be Heard by Grand Jury." *Washington Times Herald*, February 24, 1944.

———. "Mrs. Miller Gets Lind Bequest." *Washington Times Herald*, February 29, 1944.

Gabbett, Harry. "Death at Eleventh and G." *Washington Times Herald*, May 18, 1944.

———. "Lind's Killing Was Planned, Says Attorney." *Washington Times Herald*, May 17, 1944.

———. "Miller Trial Bribe Report Investigated." *Washington Times Herald*, May 20, 1944.

———. "Unshaken in Cross-Examination." *Washington Times Herald*, May 19, 1944.

Hagner, Anne. "Miller Jittery in New Type of Court Role." *Washington Post*, May 16, 1944.

Hathaway, Hanson. "Miller on Trial Tomorrow in Slaying of Lind." *Washington Times Herald*, May 14, 1944.

Kahl, Norman. "Both Sides Rap Miller's Wife in Final Argument." *Washington Evening Star*, May 31, 1944.

———. "Bribe Offer Allegation Halts Miller Murder Trial." *Washington Post*, May 20, 1944.

———. "Court Orders Jury Locked Up in Miller Trial." *Washington Evening Star*, May 19, 1944.

———. "Court Told Wife's Acts Crazed Miller." *Washington Post*, May 26, 1944.

———. "Dr. Lind Carried Gun in Envelope, Witness Says." *Washington Evening Star*, May 27, 1944.

———. "Dr. Lind's Relatives Testify He Owned Only One Revolver." *Washington Evening Star*, May 22, 1944.

———. "Fingerprint Puzzle Given Miller Jury." *Washington Post*, May 23, 1944.

———. "Government Expects to Rest Miller Case by Noon Tomorrow." *Washington Evening Star*, May 21, 1944.

———. "'I'll Get Him,' Woman Says Lind Boasted." *Washington Post*, May 25, 1944.

———. "Jury Questioning Delays Miller Murder Trial." *Washington Evening Star*, May 15, 1944.

———. "Miller, Acquitted of Dr. Lind Murder, Is Silent on Plans." *Washington Evening Star*, June 1, 1944.

———. "Miller Carried 2 Guns Before Lind Slaying, Prosecution Charges." *Washington Evening Star*, May 16, 1944.

———. "Miller Denies He Intended to Kill Dr. Lind." *Washington Evening Star*, May 26, 1944.

———. "Miller Murder Trial Judge and Attorneys Will Confer Today." *Washington Evening Star*, May 30, 1944.

———. "Miller's Friend Tells of Scuffle in Auto Before Lind Shooting." *Washington Evening Star*, May 17, 1944.

———. "Mrs. Miller Says She Paid Bills of Slain Doctor." *Washington Evening Star*, May 24, 1944.

———. "Porter Testifies Miller Threw Gun into Car." *Washington Evening Star*, May 18, 1944.

———. "Prosecutor Fihelly Testifies on Miller's Martial Difficulties." *Washington Evening Star*, May 25, 1944.

———. "Revolver Found in Lind's Car Was Doctor's Own, Welch Says." *Washington Evening Star*, May 23, 1944.

———. "Two Doctors Expected to Testify Miller Was Sane During Trial." *Washington Evening Star*, May 28, 1944.

———. "Two Psychiatrists Say Miller Was Sane on Day of Slaying." *Washington Evening Star*, May 29, 1944.

Nelson, Winifred. "How Miller Threatened Lind Told at Murder Trial." *Washington Post*, May 17, 1944.

———. "Lawyer Says He Saw Lind Gun 3 Times." *Washington Post*, May 29, 1944.

———. "Miller Calm as He Tells Jury He Shot 'Other Man.'" *Washington Post*, May 27, 1944.

———. "Miller Jury Hears Story of Shooting." *Washington Post*, May 18, 1944.

———. "Miller Trial Jurors View Lind Death Car." *Washington Post*, May 30, 1944.

———. "Miller Trial Opens; Second Panel Called." *Washington Post*, May 16, 1944.

————. "Miller Trial Witness Details 'Gun' Tossing after Shooting." *Washington Post*, May 19, 1944.

————. "Miller Triangle-Slaying Case May Reach Jury Late Today." *Washington Post*, May 31, 1944.

————. "'Not Guilty' Panel Finds, in 1 Hour, 20 Minutes." *Washington Post*, June 1, 1944.

————. "Sealed Lips of Doctor with $5000, She Asserts." *Washington Post*, May 24, 1944.

Nicholson, Roland. "'Crucified' by Wife's Trysts, Miller Sobs." *Washington Times Herald*, May 27, 1944.

————. "Defense to Call Alienists." *Washington Times Herald*, May 26, 1944.

————. "The Government Rests." *Washington Times Herald*, May 30, 1944.

————. "Government to Rest Today in Miller Case." *Washington Times Herald*, May 23, 1944.

————. "Jury Quizzes Dr. Lind's Son, Nine Others." *Washington Times Herald*, February 25, 1944.

————. "Jury Returns Verdict after 79 Minutes." *Washington Times Herald*, June 1, 1944.

————. "Kin Rally to Defense." *Washington Times Herald*, May 25, 1944.

————. "Miller's Wife Says She Paid Lind for Love." *Washington Times Herald*, May 24, 1944.

————. "Wife Wanted to Quit Miller, Doctor Says." *Washington Times Herald*, May 28, 1944.

Paull, Joseph. "Counsel Deny Miller Owned Mysterious Gun in Lind's Car." *Washington Post*, February 24, 1944.

————. "Dr. J.E. Lind Shot in Auto at Corner of 11th and G." *Washington Post*, February 22, 1944.

————. "Grand Jury Hears Lind's Son; Miller's Wife Won't Testify." *Washington Post*, February 25, 1944.

————. "Ordered Held for Action of Grand Jury after Inquest." *Washington Post*, February 23, 1944.

Strayer, Martha. "Miller Calmly Maps Own Defense, to Face Grand Jury in Slaying." *Washington Daily News*, February 23, 1944.

Time. "Crime: One of the Best." March 6, 1944.

Towe, Emily. "Mrs. Miller Met Doctor as a Patient." *Washington Post*, February 23, 1944.

U.S. Census Bureau. 1950 United States Census. Washington, D.C. Ancestry.com.

Van De Water, Marjorie. "Attempts to Take Dr. Lind's Life Reported Made by Mental Patients." *Washington Daily News*, March 10, 1944.

Ward, Veda. "Miller's Fate Will Be Handed to Jury Today." *Washington Times Herald*, May 28, 1944.

———. "Young Lind Sits by Miller's Wife but He's Alone." *Washington Times Herald*, May 28, 1944.

Washington Afro American. "Expect Porter to Be Key Witness in Miller Case." February 26, 1944.

Washington Daily News. "'Bribe' Offer Locks Up Jury Hearing Miller Murder Trial." May 20, 1944.

———. "Court Denies Appeal for the Arrest of Miller." February 29, 1944.

———. "'Crucified,' Miller Sobs on Stand." May 26, 1944.

———. "Discovery of Lind's Gun Challenges Miller Alibi." February 26, 1944.

———. "Doctor Bares Wife's Fear Miller Planned to Kill Her and Lind." May 27, 1944.

———. "Dr. Lind Owned Only 1 Pistol, Children Say at Miller Trial." May 22, 1944.

———. "Gun Ownership Probed; Jury Studies Lind Death." February 25, 1944.

———. "Inquest in Dr. Lind's Slaying Today." February 22, 1944.

———. "Installer of D.C. Death Chair, Lind Mortician Shun Miller Jury." May 16, 1944.

———. "Lind Death Struggle Described by Eye-Witness to Fatal Shots." May 18, 1944.

———. "Lind 'Hoped to Dance on Grave of Miller,' Witness Asserts." May 24, 1944.

———. "Lind Was a 'Home-Wrecker,' Ambushed to Death, Jury Told." May 31, 1944.

———. "Miller Case Is Expected to Go to the Jury Late Tomorrow." May 30, 1944.

———. "Miller, 'Changed,' Sought Advice of Fihelly in Fatal Triangle." May 25, 1944.

———. "Miller Family to Testify in Miller Trial." May 12, 1944.

———. "Miller Helps Pick Jury as Murder Trial Begins." May 15, 1944.

———. "Miller Indicted as Wife Shares in Lind's Estate." February 28, 1944.

———. "Miller Jury Ordered Locked Up at Night after Mystery Parley." May 19, 1944.

———. "Miller Pleads Not Guilty; Bond Ordered Canceled." March 6, 1944.

———. "Miller Sane as Lind Was Shot Johns Hopkins Doctor Says." May 29, 1944.

———. "Miller Unbalanced, Lawyer Says; Wife Will Take Stand Today." May 23, 1944.

———. "Miller Will Return to Practice after Murder Acquittal by Jury." June 1, 1944.

———. "Mrs. Miller First Witness in Lind Slaying Inquiry." February 24, 1944.

———. "Witness Says Miller Asked: 'Did You See Him Pull Gun on Me?'" May 17, 1944.

Washington Evening Star. "Dr. J.E. Lind Shot to Death in Car at 11th and G." February 21, 1944.

———. "Dr. Lind Described as Having Varied Talents and Interests." February 22, 1944.

———. "Dr. Lind's Residence Yields Gun Similar to One Found in Car." February 26, 1944.

———. "First-Degree Murder Indictment Is Returned Against Miller." February 28, 1944.

———. "Grand Jury Begins Taking Statements in Lind Slaying." February 24, 1944.

———. "Grand Jury Due to Act Monday in Lind Case." February 25, 1944.

———. "Judge Refuses Bench Warrant for Miller." February 29, 1944.

———. "Legends Surround Miller, Friend of Political Leaders." February 22, 1944.

———. "Lind Slaying Case Awaits Findings of Grand Jury." February 27, 1944.

———. "Lind Slaying Inquiry Centers on Two Guns and Handkerchief." February 23, 1944.

———. "Marriage Licenses." October 18, 1928.

———. "Miller Case Witness Admits Fake on 'Bribe.'" July 11, 1944.

———. "Miller Insanity Plea Indicated by Visit of Two Psychiatrists." May 11, 1944.

———. "Miller Is Held for Grand Jury after Inquest." February 22, 1944.

———. "Miller Trial Figure Who Told of 'Bribe' Indicted for Perjury." June 29, 1944.

———. "Prosecution Calls 50 for Miller Trial Opening Monday." May 12, 1944.

———. "Trial of Robert Miller in Dr. Lind Slaying to Start Tomorrow." May 14, 1944.

———. "Yow Is Sentenced to Year for Miller Trial Bribe Tale." July 14, 1944.

Washington Herald. "Robert Ingersoll Miller." February 18, 1921.

Washington Post. "Arraignment of Miller Due Tomorrow." March 3, 1944.

———. "1st Degree Murder Indictment Is Returned Against Miller." February 29, 1944.

———. "Indictment Echo of Miller Murder Trial." June 30, 1944.

———. "Love-Slaying Probers Find Third Gun at Dr. Lind's Home." February 26, 1944.

———. "Miller Jury Voted 'Not Guilty' on 1st Ballot after 10 Minutes." June 2, 1944.

———. "Miller Likely to Stay in Jail, Green Says." March 8, 1944.

———. "Miller Ordered Jailed by Court." March 7, 1944.

———. "Miller Ready for Trial Today in Lind Slaying." May 15, 1944.

———. "Miller Resumes Law Practice, Wins Larceny Case for Client." June 3, 1944.

———. "Miller's Fate to Be Decided This Week." May 29, 1944.

———. "Miller Trial Prosecution to Rest Today." May 22, 1944.

———. "Slain Doctor's Funeral Today; 2 Sons Arrive." February 24, 1944.

Washington Times Herald. "Kin of Lind Take Stand Today at Trial of Miller." May 22, 1944.

———. "Lind Jury May Act Tomorrow." February 27, 1944.

———. "Miller Awaits Decision Today by Grand Jury." February 29, 1944.

———. "Miller's Story Faces Attack." May 29, 1944.

———. "Miller to Return to Law Practice after Recovery." June 2, 1944.

———. "Miller Trial Opens Today." May 15, 1944.

Wissman, Bert. "Noonday Trysts of Mrs. Miller and Lind Bared." *Washington Times Herald*, February 24, 1944.

Chapter 4

Allen, Robert. "Slain Woman Found Joy in Solitude." *Washington Post*, March 3, 1944.

Epstein, Sidney, and Dwight Martin. "Carol's Slayer Hasn't Told All, Detectives Declare after Grilling." *Washington Times Herald*, July 10, 1948.

Fisher v. United States, 328 U.S. 463 (1946).

Fitzgerald, Russell. "Murder Victim Buried in Rain at Alexandria." *Washington Times Herald*, March 5, 1944.

Gabbett, Harry. "Jurors View Death Room at Cathedral." *Washington Times Herald*, June 27, 1944.

————. "3 Diagnoses of Fisher's Mind Given at Trial." *Washington Times Herald*, June 29, 1944.

Green, Allen. "Confessed Cathedral Slayer Calm at His Arraignment." *Washington Daily News*, March 3, 1944.

Keedy, Edwin. "A Problem of First Degree Murder: Fisher v. United States." *University of Pennsylvania Law Review* 99, no. 3 (1950): 267–92.

Michigan Chronicle (Detroit, MI). "Charles Houston Named to Replace P.B. Young on FEPC." March 4, 1944.

————. "Houston Quits FEPC; Raps President Truman." December 8, 1945.

Northern Virginia Daily. "Librarian's Body Found Battered in Big Cathedral." March 3, 1944.

Pollock, Laura. "Question of Evidence." *Washington Post*, December 15, 1946.

Reiff, Jean. "Cathedral Slayer Found Guilty after 40 Minutes' Deliberation." *Washington Post*, June 30, 1944.

————. "Doctors Lay Cathedral Killing to 'Insane Impulse,' 'Rage.'" *Washington Post*, June 29, 1944.

————. "Fisher Tells of Strangling, Clubbing Librarian to Death." *Washington Post*, June 28, 1944.

————. "Jury Visits Cathedral Library Where Miss Reardon Was Slain." *Washington Post*, June 27, 1944.

Richmond Times-Dispatch. "Graduate of W&M Slain in Washington." March 3, 1944.

————. "Miss Reardon Known as 'Good Student.'" March 2, 1944.

Siegel, David. "Felix Frankfurter, Charles Hamilton Houston and the 'N-Word': A Case Study in the Evolution of Judicial Attitudes Toward Race." *Southern California Interdisciplinary Law Journal* 7, no. 2 (1998): 317 73.

Singerhoff, John. "Bloodstained Clothes Lead to Arrest of Employee." *Washington Post*, March 3, 1944.

Talty, Edward, and James Walter. "Janitor, 34, Slew Woman over Reproof." *Washington Times Herald*, March 3, 1944.

Taylor, Herman. "Partial Insanity as Affecting the Degree of Crime: A Commentary on *Fisher v. United States*." *California Law Review* 34, no. 4 (1946): 625–43.

Ward, Veda. "Never Intended to Kill Librarian, Fisher Testifies." *Washington Times Herald*, June 28, 1944.

Washington Afro American. "Wife of Cathedral Murder Suspect Believes in Him." March 11, 1944.

Washington Daily News. "Cathedral Librarian Fought for Life, Testimony Shows." June 27, 1944.

———. "8 Women on Jury Trying Cathedral Murder Case." June 26, 1944.

———. "Grand Jury to Hear Cathedral Case Monday." March 4, 1944.

———. "Janitor Admits Slitting Throat of Cathedral Librarian." June 28, 1944.

———. "Late Testimony Delays Cathedral Murder Trial." June 30, 1944.

———. "Woman Found Slain at Cathedral Here." March 2, 1944.

Washington Evening Star. "Cathedral Handyman Indicted on 6 Counts in Reardon Slaying." March 6, 1944.

———. "Cathedral Library Slayer Is Given Another Stay." April 19, 1945.

———. "Cathedral Murderer Will Die November 29." October 23, 1946.

———. "Cathedral Slayer's Execution Postponed." June 20, 1946.

———. "'Cathedral Slayer' Wins Eighth Postponement." May 3, 1946.

———. "Clemency Denied Fisher; 3 Executions Set Dec. 20." December 11, 1946.

———. "Confession Goes into Record at Fisher Trial." June 27, 1944.

———. "Coroner's Jury Holds Janitor in Reardon Slaying." March 3, 1944.

———. "Court Denies Motion for Doomed Slayers as Jail Witnesses." July 11, 1946.

———. "Execution of Medley, 2 Others Postponed by District Court." November 18, 1946.

———. "Fisher Execution Awaits High Court Decision." March 8, 1946.

———. "Fisher Execution Delayed Pending High Court Ruling." August 17, 1946.

———. "Fisher Is Sentenced to Die Nov. 24 in Cathedral Slaying." July 7, 1944.

———. "Fisher Loses Appeal on Death Sentence in Cathedral Slaying." April 23, 1945.

———. "Fisher Wins Review in Death Sentence for Cathedral Slaying." October 9, 1945.

———. "Funeral Is Conducted for Miss Courtenay." April 5, 1937.

———. "Grand Jury Expected to Study Cathedral Slaying Case Monday." March 3, 1944.

———. "Julius Fisher Execution Postponed Sixth Time." January 17, 1946.

———. "Jury to Visit Slaying Scene at Cathedral." June 26, 1944.

———. "Medley Had Turned to Religion for Solace, Chaplain Discloses." December 20, 1946.

———. "Medley Is Given Rites of Church at Mount Olivet." December 22, 1946.

———. "Medley's Death Delayed 2 Hours by Final Pleas." December 20, 1946.

———. "Mergner and Fisher Executions Delayed." November 8, 1944.

———. "Mergner, Fisher Win Stays of Execution." June 15, 1945.

———. "Mrs. Reardon, Mother of Slain Librarian, Dies." December 4, 1944.

———. "Reardon Slayer Faces Arraignment Friday." March 7, 1944.

———. "Supreme Court Balks Medley and Fisher on Execution Appeals." June 11, 1946.

———. "Supreme Court Rejects Medley and Fisher Appeals for Rehearing." October 14, 1946.

———. "Trial Set Tomorrow in Cathedral Slaying." June 25, 1944.

———. "Two Prosecutors Named in Reardon Slaying Case." March 18, 1944.

———. "Two Who Passed Up Opportunity to Flee Death House Lauded." April 6, 1946.

———. "2 Young Women End Lives by Gas in Suicide Pact." April 2, 1937.

———. "Woman Library Aide Beaten to Death in Cathedral Building." March 2, 1944.

Washington Post. "Arraignment in Cathedral Death Delayed." March 11, 1944.

———. "Attorney Seeks New Trial for Cathedral Slayer." July 2, 1944.

———. "Case for Commutation." June 22, 1946.

———. "Execution of Fisher Set for Nov. 24." July 8, 1944.

———. "Final Appeal Denied, Medley to Die Today." December 20, 1946.

———. "Library Is Gift of Mrs. Janin; Honors Parent." March 3, 1944.

———. "Medley and Fisher Appeals Rejected by Supreme Court." June 11, 1946.

———. "Plea of Not Guilty Made by Fisher in Cathedral Death." March 19, 1944.

———. "Suspect in Slaying Held for Grand Jury." March 4, 1944.

———. "3 Executions Stayed Pending Plea Verdicts." January 9, 1945.

———. "Truman Denies Clemency to 2 Murderers." November 28, 1946.

———. "2 Slayers Lose High Court Pleas." October 15, 1946.

Washington Times. "Mother Comes Here to Claim Girl's Body." April 5, 1937.

Washington Times Herald. "Fisher Guilty of Murdering Catherine Reardon, Gets Chair." June 30, 1944.

————. "Library Slaying Laid to Pent-Up Rage at Rebukes." March 4, 1944.

————. "Miss Reardon Had Feared Lonely 'Crypt.'" March 3, 1944.

Weihofen, Henry, and Winfred Overholser. "Mental Disorder Affecting the Degree of a Crime." *Yale Law Journal* 56, no. 6 (1947): 959–81.

Wright, Richard. "The Man Who Killed a Shadow." In *Eight Men*, 185–202. New York: HarperPerennial, 1996.

Yarbrough, Charles. "Death Hour Delayed by Futile Court Maneuver." *Washington Post*, December 21, 1946.

Young, Joseph. "Final Arguments Slated Today in Cathedral Death." *Washington Evening Star*, June 29, 1944.

————. "Fisher Awaits Sentencing to Electric Chair." *Washington Evening Star*, June 30, 1944.

————. "Fisher Denies Premeditation in Slaying." *Washington Evening Star*, June 28, 1944.

————. "U.S. Due to Conclude Evidence Today in Cathedral Slaying." *Washington Evening Star*, June 27, 1944.

Chapter 5

Baltimore Evening Sun. "Brill." July 7, 1948.

————. "Court of Appeals Rules James Must Hang." April 27, 1949.

————. "'Demented' Man Being Quizzed in Brill Case." July 8, 1948.

————. "Efforts to Introduce James 'Confession' Balked at Trial." September 21, 1948.

————. "Eugene James Appeals Death Sentence." January 7, 1949.

————. "Girl, 11, Knifed to Death Here: Man Hunt On." July 6, 1948.

————. "Hundreds Attend Brill Funeral." July 8, 1948.

————. "James Asks New Trial in Brill Murder." September 24, 1948.

————. "James Case Witnesses Called by Prosecution." September 13, 1948.

————. "James Doomed for Slaying of Marsha Brill." November 10, 1948.

————. "James Indicted in D.C. Girl's Knife Death." July 19, 1948.

————. "James Is Denied New Trial by Court." November 6, 1948.

————. "Janitor Is Charged in Marsha Brill Knife Slaying." July 9, 1948.

————. "Janitor Offers Insanity Plea in Slaying." July 13, 1948.

————. "Marsha's Playmate Points to James as 'The Man.'" September 20, 1948.

———. "Mental Test Ordered for James." July 27, 1948.

———. "'Mental Torture' Is Charged in James Case." March 29, 1949.

———. "Murder in First Degree Is Verdict." September 22, 1948.

———. "Policemen Cited for Brill Case Performance." July 10, 1948.

———. "State Drops Case Against James." November 15, 1948.

———. "3 Psychiatrists to Study James." July 15, 1948.

———. "Trial of James Is Postponed to Sept. 20." July 21, 1948.

———. "2 More Arrested in Search for Slayer." July 7, 1948.

Baltimore Sun. "Appeals Court Voids Crime News Rules, Lifts Contempt Fines." June 10, 1949.

———. "Brill Case Confession Is Admitted." September 22, 1948.

———. "City Judges Are Criticized." July 8, 1948.

———. "Court Cites 5 Radio Stations for Contempt." July 21, 1948.

———. "Girl Bicyclist Stabbed to Death; 2 Men Held for Questioning in Case." July 7, 1948.

———. "Girl Slaying Is Charged to Janitor." July 9, 1948.

———. "James Given Death Penalty." November 11, 1948.

———. "James Is Hanged for Brill Murder." August 12, 1949.

———. "James Seen with Knife, Court Told." September 21, 1948.

———. "James to Get Sentence for Killing Child." November 7, 1948.

———. "James to Hang August 12 for Brill Murder." July 20, 1948.

———. "Judge Finds James Guilty of Murder." September 23, 1948.

———. "Man in Lineup Is Grilled in Girl's Slaying." July 8, 1948.

———. "New Trial Asked for Eugene James." September 25, 1948.

———. "2d Murder Laid to Brill Case Suspect." July 14, 1948.

Bardwell, Betty. "A Message from Carol's Mother." *Washington Times Herald*, July 7, 1948.

Davis, Charles. "James Found Guilty in Brill Girl's Murder." *Washington Post*, September 23, 1948.

———. "Slain Child's Friend Points Out James." *Washington Post*, September 21, 1948.

Dempsey, Margaret. "Marsha Brill Was 'So Nice, Even to Her Little Sister.'" July 7, 1948.

Epstein, Sidney. "Escapes Cops in Rock Creek Night Search." *Washington Times Herald*, July 8, 1948.

———. "Janitor Admits Killing Baltimore Child." *Washington Times Herald*, July 9, 1948.

———. "Second Cyclist Killed by Knife; Suspects Held." *Washington Times Herald*, July 7, 1948.

———. "Tests by FBI Hint Slain Girl Sex Victim." *Washington Times Herald*, June 30, 1948.

Horner, John. "Baltimore 'Gag' Appears Certain of Court Test." *Washington Evening Star*, July 22, 1948.

Jacobs, Bradford. "Silent, Tense Group of 18 Sees Two Executions." *Baltimore Evening Sun*, August 12, 1949.

Keats, John. "Lawyers Battle Over Confession in James Trial." *Washington Daily News*, September 21, 1948.

Lansner, Herbert. "Crime Week Old, but Girl's Killer Is Still at Large." *Washington Times Herald*, July 4, 1948.

Marder, Murrey. "Baltimore Press Chafes at Crime News Handcuffs." July 18, 1948.

———. "Baltimore Radio Stations Cited for Contempt in James Case." July 21, 1948.

Matthews, Ralph. "Doubt Janitor Killed Girl." *Washington Afro American*, July 24, 1948.

O'Donnell, Maureen. "Maryland Reviews Its Law on Secrecy of Execution Date." *Washington Times*, n.d.

Reiff, Jean. "No Progress Made in Girl Murder Case." *Washington Post*, July 6, 1948.

———. "Park and City Police Gear on Major Crime." *Washington Post*, July 4, 1948.

Walter, James. "Confession Trumped Up." *Washington Times Herald*, July 14, 1948.

———. "Grand Jurors Get Bardwell Slaying Today." *Washington Times Herald*, July 15, 1948.

Washington Afro American. "Baffled Police Stir Protests." July 10, 1948.

———. "How Riots Are Made." July 3, 1948.

———. "Police to Mark Case 'Closed.'" October 2, 1948.

Washington Daily News. "Baltimore Slaying Yields No Clues to Bardwell Case." July 7, 1948.

———. "Barrett Believes Baltimore Killer Slew Carol, Too." July 8, 1948.

———. "Chief Barratt Believes: 3 Young Girls Key to Child's Murder." June 29, 1948.

———. "Cops' Case Against Janitor Bolstered by Two Witnesses." July 14, 1948.

———. "Cops Checking Gaps in Janitor's Story." July 10, 1948.

———. "Few Clues Left in Child's Murder." July 2, 1948.

———. "Grand Jury Awaiting Blood Test Report in Bardwell Case." July 16, 1948.

———. "Grand Jury Indicts James for Carol Bardwell's Murder." July 19, 1948.

———. "Grand Jury to Hear Evidence in Slaying." July 13, 1948.

———. "Homicide Men Return to Baltimore in Killing." July 12, 1948.

———. "In Loving Memory." August 11, 1948.

———. "James Seen 'Coming and Going' on Freight." July 15, 1948.

———. "Last Clue Is Run Out; Slaying Still Unsolved." July 3, 1948.

———. "Police at Dead-End after Week's Hunt for Child's Slayer." July 5, 1948.

———. "Police Say Carol Knew Her Attacker." July 1, 1948.

———. "Police Seek Trace of Bloody Hitchhiker." June 30, 1948.

———. "Sex Maniac Hunted in Slaying of Girl, 11." June 28, 1948.

Washington Evening Star. "Baltimore Contempt Cases." July 22, 1948.

———. "Baltimore Junior Bar Group Enters Radio Contempt Case." September 10, 1948.

———. "Baltimore Man Admits He Killed Carol Bardwell." July 9, 1948.

———. "Baltimore 'Press Gag' on Crime News Called 'Repugnant' by ANPA." January 19, 1949.

———. "Bardwell, Carol Elizabeth." June 29, 1948.

———. "Bardwell Case Cited by Writers Opposing Maryland Press Curb." July 12, 1948.

———. "Bardwell Case Is Nearing End for Grand Jury." July 16, 1948.

———. "Bardwells Give Hospital Picture in Girl's Memory." August 11, 1948.

———. "Both Sides Rest at James Trial in Brill Slaying." September 22, 1948.

———. "Calls for 'Strong Action' as Police Piece Out Story of Girl's Slaying." July 11, 1948.

———. "Caught—But Too Late." July 10, 1948.

———. "Citizen Group Offers Reward for Slayer." July 2, 1948.

———. "Civil Liberties Groups Enter Radio Trial." January 20, 1949.

———. "Completed Autopsy Reveals Slain Girl Had Been Assaulted." June 30, 1948.

———. "Court Denies New Trial to James in Slaying of Baltimore Girl." November 7, 1948.

———. "Court's Authority Cited in Baltimore 'News Gag' Case." October 16, 1948.

———. "Crossing Guard Says She Saw James on Train." July 15, 1948.

———. "Curb on Crime News Attacked, Defended at Baltimore Trial." January 26, 1949.

———. "D.C. Detectives Seek to Sew Up Bardwell Case." July 12, 1948.

———. "D.C. Police to Seek Early Indictment in Bardwell Slaying." July 10, 1948.

———. "Delay Asked in Replies to Contempt Citations Till after James' Trial." July 25, 1948.

———. "First-Degree Verdict Handed Down Against James in Murder Case." September 22, 1948.

———. "5 Baltimore Stations to Reply by August 16 in Contempt Citation." July 21, 1948.

———. "Fly Says Baltimore 'Gag' Abridges Free Press." July 29, 1948.

———. "Gallows Noose Slips as James Is Executed for Murdering Girl." August 12, 1949.

———. "Hard, Tedious Work Makes Murray Detective Chief." August 28, 1950.

———. "Inadequate Park Patrol." July 1, 1948.

———. "James Appeals Conviction in Slaying of Brill Girl." November 19, 1948.

———. "James Asks New Trial in Brill Girl Slaying." September 24, 1948.

———. "James Indicted in Slaying of Carol Bardwell." July 19, 1948.

———. "James Is Sentenced to Hang for Murder." November 10, 1948.

———. "James to Go On Trial in Baltimore Tomorrow." September 19, 1948.

———. "James to Hang Aug. 12 for Slaying Brill Girl." July 20, 1949.

———. "James to Hang Tonight for Slaying Girl, 11; Knowles Also to Die." August 11, 1949.

———. "Janitor Looks Like Brill Killer, Witness Says." September 20, 1948.

———. "Janitor's Trial Opens in Killing of Brill Girl." September 20, 1948.

———. "Judge Gray to Preside in News Censorship Contempt Proceedings." November 18, 1948.

———. "Jury Will Get Bardwell Killing Scene Diagram." July 14, 1948.

———. "Man Posing as Solicitor of Bardwell Fund Sought." July 18, 1948.

———. "Maryland Court Hears Opposition to Curb on Crime Reports." May 19, 1949.

———. "Murray Named to Command D.C. Detectives." August 24, 1950.

———. "Newspaper Officials to Discuss Maryland Press Gag Proposal." July 28, 1948.

———. "Park Murder Solution Still Far Off Despite Questioning of 100." July 2, 1948.

———. "Police and Citizens Increase Rewards for Slayer of Girl." July 3, 1948.

———. "Police Seek 3 Girls Seen Hurrying from Park after Slaying." June 29, 1948.

———. "Police Seek to Link Slaying in Baltimore with Bardwell Case." July 7, 1948.

———. "Police Still Seek Clue in Murder of Girl in Park." June 28, 1948.

———. "Police Try to Fill Gaps in Story of Bardwell Killing." July 11, 1948.

———. "Police Watch Scene in Hope Bardwell Slayer May Return." July 5, 1948.

———. "Press and Radio Hail Reversal of Court Curb in Baltimore." June 10, 1949.

———. "Radio Stations' Trial for Contempt Set for Jan. 27 in Baltimore." December 17, 1948.

———. "Rites for Slain Girl Conducted as Hunt for Killer Continues." July 1, 1948.

———. "Same Man Killed Girls Here and in Baltimore, Maj. Barrett Believes." July 8, 1948.

———. "Sentence Awaits James' Appeal in Murder of Girl." September 23, 1948.

———. "Supreme Court Ruling on Press 'Gag' Leaves Questions, Warnings." January 10, 1950.

———. "Three Girls Provide No Clues in Slaying of Carol Bardwell." July 6, 1948.

———. "Two Policemen Tell How James Disclosed Knife." September 21, 1948.

———. "Will Speed Bardwell Case to Grand Jury." July 13, 1948.

———. "Woman's Assailant Sought for Grilling in Bardwell Case." July 4, 1948.

Washington Post. "Accused Slayer's Trial Set Monday." September 14, 1948.

———. "Baltimore Gag Rule." July 15, 1948.

———. "Bardwell Case Suspect Flees as Police Fire." July 8, 1948.

———. "Bardwell Murder Case Week Old and Police Still Baffled." July 4, 1948.

———. "Carol Bardwell Slayer Suspect Will Hang Friday." August 11, 1949.

———. "Citizens Asked to Aid Hunt for Girl Killer." July 1, 1948.

————. "Court Orders Mental Test for James in Knife Slaying." July 28, 1948.

————. "Court Upholds Death Sentence of James in Killing of Girl, 11." April 28, 1949.

————. "D.C. Girl, 11, Murdered in Rock Creek." June 28, 1948.

————. "Death Sentence Given James in Murder of Girl." November 11, 1948.

————. "Detectives Sent to Baltimore in Girl's Death." July 7, 1948.

————. "District Attorney to Receive Bardwell Case Evidence Today." July 12, 1948.

————. "Ex-Convict Confesses Bardwell Girl Slaying." July 10, 1948.

————. "Fund Voted to Add 40 to Park Police." March 29, 1949.

————. "Good Work." July 10, 1948.

————. "James Appeals Death Sentence for Girl's Death." January 9, 1949.

————. "James Confession Admitted in Trial." September 22, 1948.

————. "James Denied New Trial in Brill Slaying." November 7, 1948.

————. "James on Trial for Baltimore Girl's Slaying." September 20, 1948.

————. "James Will Hang after Midnight." August 12, 1949.

————. "Janitor Accused in 2 Girls' Deaths on Trial Monday." September 16, 1948.

————. "Jury Indicts Janitor in Bardwell Park Slaying." July 20, 1948.

————. "Jury to Hear Case Against James Today." July 15, 1948.

————. "Known Sex Offenders." July 17, 1948.

————. "Man Found Prowling Near Murder Scene." July 2, 1948.

————. "Md. Slayer Questioned on Bardwell Case." July 9, 1948.

————. "Murder in the Park." June 30, 1948.

————. "New Trial Plea in Brill Slaying to Be Heard Today." November 6, 1948.

————. "Noose Slips, James Dies by Strangling." August 13, 1949.

————. "Park View Playground Plan Scored." July 8, 1948.

————. "Police Confer on James Case in Baltimore." July 13, 1948.

————. "Police Seeking More Evidence in Slaying of Bardwell Girl." July 17, 1948.

————. "Police Sure Janitor Is Girl's Slayer." July 14, 1948.

————. "'Psychological Torture' Made James Defense." March 30, 1949.

————. "Puppy, Cocker, Setter 'Bought to Protect' Area Wake It Up; Self-Muzzling Ordered." June 18, 1949.

————. "Railroad Crossing 'Watchwoman' Tells of Seeing James Riding Freight." July 16, 1948.

————. "Rock Creek Park Police Watch Section Where Girl Was Slain." July 5, 1948.

————. "Sex Perverts Invade D.C., House Told." July 30, 1948.

————. "Slayer of Girl, 11, May Win Appeal at State Expense." November 24, 1948.

————. "3 Baltimore Radio Stations Found Guilty Under 'Gag' Rule." January 29, 1949.

————. "Three Questioned in Slaying of Girl in Rock Creek Park." June 29, 1948.

————. "3 Young Girls Sought in Park Slaying." June 30, 1948.

————. "Trail Fades in Hunt for Girl Slayer." July 3, 1948.

————. "Trial Set Monday in Girl's Murder." September 19, 1948.

————. "Woman Keen on Railroad Crossing Job." July 18, 1948.

Washington Times Herald. "Army Sleuths Join Hunt for Girl's Killer." June 29, 1948.

————. "Carol's Slayer Must Hang for Murder in Md." November 11, 1948.

————. "Clues Fading in Search for Carol's Killer." July 5, 1948.

————. "D.C. Posts $300 for Girl's Killer." July 3, 1948.

————. "From Gov. Lane." July 24, 1948.

————. "Is Real Slayer at Large?" July 13, 1948.

————. "James Indicted for Bardwell Girl's Murder." July 20, 1948.

————. "Park Hunt Centers on Boy, Man." July 1, 1948.

————. "Police Merger Sought in War Upon Perverts." July 30, 1948.

————. "Remon Assails James Parole; Feted at Dinner." July 15, 1948.

————. "Sex Maniac Slays Girl, 11, in Park Here." June 28, 1948.

————. "Sex Slayer Admitted Carol's Murder First; Discrepancies Probed." July 11, 1948.

————. "Spotted James on Day Carol Was Murdered, Two Women Tell Jury." July 16, 1948.

————. "Unequal Justice?" July 13, 1948.

Whitman, Howard. "Terror in Washington." *Washington Post*, June 18, 1950.

Chapter 6

Commonwealth of Pennsylvania. Application for World War II Compensation form for Stanley Szary, June 6, 1950. Ancestry.com.

Gorski, Julian. "Bolling GI Beats Wife to Death with Fists." *Washington Times Herald*, February 26, 1951.

Hayes, Gregory. "$1,000 Fine in Fatal Beating Too Puny, Says Rep. Brooks." *Washington Times Herald*, September 29, 1951.

Shreveport Journal. "Fine Airman $1,000 for Killing Wife." September 28, 1951.

———. "Mate Held after Death of Former Local Woman." February 26, 1951.

———. "Miscarriage of Justice?" January 30, 1952.

Times (Shreveport, LA). "Husband Held in Death of Shreveport Woman." February 26, 1951.

U.S. Congress. *Congressional Record.* 82nd Cong., 1st sess., 1951. Vol. 97, pt. 15.

U.S. Department of War. Draft Registration Card for Stanley Szary, October 16, 1940. Ancestry.com.

Valley Independent (Monessen, PA). "Stanley Szary." February 8, 2001.

Washington Daily News. "GI Fined $1000 for Killing Wife." June 29, 1951.

———. "Sergeant Indicted in Wife Slaying." March 19, 1951.

———. "Sergt. Held in Killing of Wife." February 26, 1951.

Washington Evening Star. "Bolling Base Sergeant Is Fined $1,000 in Fatal Beating of Wife." June 29, 1951.

———. "Congress Gets Protest in Case of GI Fined in Wife's Slaying." September 29, 1951.

———. "Inquest Holds Bolling Airman in Wife's Death." February 26, 1951.

———. "Jury Indicts Airman in Fatal Wife Beating." March 20, 1951.

———. "Sargeant [*sic*] Pleads Guilty to Manslaughter in Beating." June 4, 1951.

Washington Post. "Airman Held for Jury in Wife's Death." February 27, 1951.

———. "Airman Pleads Guilty in Fatal Beating of Wife." June 5, 1951.

———. "Five Years for Burglar Who Stole to Get Dope." June 30, 1951.

———. "Probe Asked in Action on Slaying Here." September 29, 1951.

———. "Two Held for Trial in 2d-Degree Murder." March 20, 1951.

———. "Wife Beaten to Death." February 26, 1951.

Washington Times Herald. "Charge of Murder Holds GI in Fist-Slaying of His Wife." February 27, 1951.

Chapter 7

Berliner, Milton. "Did Mrs. Mullis Set Out to Kill?" *Washington Daily News*, September 24, 1958.

———. "'I Don't Know What Was the Matter.'" *Washington Daily News*, September 22, 1958.

———. "Mrs. Mullis Weeps on Stand." *Washington Daily News*, September 23, 1958.

———. "She Saw Her Husband and a Lady…" *Washington Daily News*, September 18, 1958.

———. "Slayers Sent to St. E's." *Washington Daily News*, September 26, 1958.

———. "Was She Shedding Tears for Herself?" *Washington Daily News*, September 25, 1958.

———. "'We Knew People Wouldn't Accept This.'" *Washington Daily News*, September 19, 1958.

Clayton, James. "Insanity Defense Procedure in District Attacked." *Washington Post*, September 29, 1958.

———. "Mrs. Mullis Acquitted, Held Insane." *Washington Post*, September 26, 1958.

———. "Mullis." *Washington Post*, September 19, 1958.

———. "Mullis Case Set for Jury Today." *Washington Post*, September 25, 1958.

———. "Psychiatrist Testifies at Mrs. Mullis' Trial." *Washington Post*, September 24, 1958.

Commonwealth of Virginia. Death Certificate for Onie Mullis, August 23, 1962. Ancestry.com.

Dunie, Morrey. "Wife Testifies in Mullis Case." *Washington Post*, September 23, 1958.

Elder, Shirley. "She Took a Samurai Letter-Opener 'In Case of Trouble,' and Found It." *Northern Virginia Sun*, April 29, 1958.

Northern Virginia Sun. "Arlington Housewife Faces Murder Charge." April 28, 1958.

———. "Bond Asked by Woman in Slaying." April 29, 1958.

———. "Indict Arlington Woman in Slaying." May 13, 1958.

———. "Mrs. Mullis Acquitted on Insanity Plea." September 26, 1958.

———. "Mrs. Mullis Free." May 5, 1958.

———. "Onie Mullis Asks for Her Freedom." October 14, 1958.

———. "Onie Mullis Gets Release." April 17, 1959.

State of North Carolina. Divorce Certificate for Onie Mullis, August 21, 1961. Ancestry.com.

Thomas, Phil. "'All Mixed Up,' Declares Woman at Slaying Trial." *Washington Evening Star*, September 23, 1958.

———. "Errant Spouse Calls Mate 'Flawless Wife.'" *Washington Evening Star*, September 19, 1958.

———. "Prosecution Sums Up at Mrs. Mullis' Trial." *Washington Evening Star*, September 24, 1958.

———. "Slayer Asks for Freedom." *Washington Evening Star*, September 30, 1958.

———. "Slayer Likely to Stay Six Months in Hospital." *Washington Evening Star*, September 26, 1958.

Times-Tribune (Scranton, PA). "Final Rites Tomorrow for Stabbing Victim." April 30, 1958.

———. "Miss Kathryn Joyce, 30, Ex-Scrantonian, Is Slain." April 28, 1958.

———. "Rites Conducted for Stab Victim." May 1, 1958.

Washington Daily News. "Insanity Plea Set in Stabbing." September 17, 1958.

———. "Mrs. Mullis Requests Competency Hearing." September 30, 1958.

———. "Mrs. Mullis Wins Partial Freedom." April 16, 1959.

———. "Wife Held in Stabbing Here." April 28, 1958.

———. "Won't Free Mrs. Mullis." October 18, 1958.

Washington Evening Star. "Bond Allowed in Murder Case." May 2, 1958.

———. "Hearing Slated on Mrs. Mullis' Bid for Release." October 11, 1958.

———. "Husband Says Stabbing Was Like 'Dream.'" September 22, 1958.

———. "Jury Told Mrs. Mullis Was Insane." September 18, 1958.

———. "Mrs. Mullis Granted Conditional Release." April 16, 1959.

———. "Mrs. Mullis Loses Plea for Release." October 18, 1958.

———. "Slaying Jury Gets Story of Wife's Arrest." September 17, 1958.

———. "Wife Who Slew Rival Awaits Jury Verdict." September 25, 1958.

Washington Post. "Bond Granted Mrs. Mullis by Holtzoff." May 3, 1958.

———. "Hearing Set Friday on Onie Mullis Plea." October 11, 1958.

———. "Indictment Names Wife in Slaying." May 13, 1958.

———. "Inquest Holds Wife in Knifing." April 29, 1958.

———. "Inquest Slated Tuesday in Clerk-Typist Slaying." April 28, 1958.

———. "Jury Picked to Try Wife in Slaying." September 17, 1958.

———. "Mrs. Mullis Jury Told of Slaying." September 18, 1958.

———. "Mrs. Mullis Loses Plea to Leave St. Elizabeths." October 18, 1958.

———. "Mrs. Mullis' Release Asked." September 30, 1958.

———. "Onie Mullis Is Released Conditionally." April 17, 1959.

———. "St. Elizabeth's Would Free Onie Mullis." April 16, 1959.

———. "Woman Slain; Housewife Held." April 27, 1958.

ABOUT THE AUTHOR

 **Z**achary G. Ford is a high school English teacher in Fairfax, Virginia, and an officer in the U.S. Army Reserve. He holds degrees from the University of Texas and Temple University. In his spare time, he enjoys exploring the historic sites of the world and continuing his true crime research.

Visit us at
www.historypress.com